Christian Education
Where the Learning Is

Christian Education
Where the Learning Is

VIRGIL E. FOSTER

PRENTICE-HALL, INC.
Englewood Cliffs, New Jersey

PRENTICE-HALL INTERNATIONAL, INC., *London*
PRENTICE-HALL OF AUSTRALIA, PTY. LTD., *Sydney*
PRENTICE-HALL OF CANADA, LTD., *Toronto*
PRENTICE-HALL OF INDIA PRIVATE LTD., *New Delhi*
PRENTICE-HALL OF JAPAN, INC., *Tokyo*

© 1968 by
PRENTICE-HALL, INC.
Englewood Cliffs, N.J.

Library of Congress Catalog Card No.: 68-15349

Current printing (*last number*):

10 9 8 7 6 5 4 3 2 1

Printed in the United States of America

to
the teachers and students
with whom I have been associated
and who have taught me
much more than I have taught them

Preface

This is a time of tremendous advancement in opportunities for Christian education. We have the knowledge, equipment, and materials for improving Christian education more than ever before, for more people, in relation to more areas of life and responsibility. It is a time, also, of revolutionary developments in the church's theological engagement, its re-examination of all aspects of education, and its honest facing of its ecumenical nature, affecting everything we do in Christian education.

Critical issues of the world have come to the front in Christian thinking and must occupy a prominent place in Christian education in the years ahead. We hear much about the explosion of knowledge, especially in scientific fields, but we must not overlook the tremendous expansion of knowledge in the field of religion and the increased communication between leaders of the church and those in other fields of knowledge. These developments contribute to a new educational atmosphere in which the church must work.

There is a new burst of interest in Christian education of adults. Experiments are being conducted with new groupings of students and with the scheduling of Christian education throughout the week rather than on Sunday morning only. There have been some amazing discoveries of the capacity for learning and comprehension at a very early age. Experiments are being conducted in speeding up learning, instruments for programed instruction are being developed and tested, and there are new developments in the educational use of mass media and audio-visual and pictorial materials. Capacity of handicapped persons to learn, live, and participate in the common life has been found to be greater than had been assumed. The emergence of a greater margin of leisure presents Christian educators with a responsibility and opportunity to become a vital part of the lives of people. In the face of these and other circumstances, most of the denominations are working harder than ever before in the development of new curriculum and reference materials and in leadership education.

In many ways the present program of Christian education is inadequate, and this fact signals the need for churches to remake it as radically as may be necessary into a more effective educational ministry. The future has great promise if we can see it. With all the help that denominations, working singly or cooperatively, can give their churches, however, Christian education comes into existence in the local church and community. That is where the education has to happen.

A church can "pass by on the other side," ignoring the changes that are taking place, or it can be a part of the changes and play a significant role in enlarging the lives of its people. It has the opportunity to be a part of the new Christian education as it develops. Its people can have enjoyment and excitement in helping their church be a significant factor in the lives of human beings— their friends and neighbors—who are trying to understand what is happening to them in the world and what they can do about it.

It is not a lack of Christian education materials that keeps many churches from having the kind of education program needed. It is, rather, the fact that the leaders do not understand where and how learning takes place and what they need to do to make Christian education effective.

This book indicates some of the many areas in which learning takes place and in which Christian education can happen. In most instances changes in Christian education will take place only as there is aggressive planning to bring them about. In going through each chapter the reader may well keep before him always the question, "What is my church doing about this?" He may want to make notes about things he can do to initiate study and action in his church. Then he can share the book with others, starting discussions about the development of the kind of educational program needed.

This does not mean that every church will establish exactly the same kind of educational program. Efforts will vary from church to church, according to specific needs and resources.

The opportunities for Christian education are so great and the need for it so urgent that every church should set up a Christian education board, commission, or committee if it does not have one, to explore the needs and resources, evaluate the present program, and begin the action needed to develop an effective educational ministry.

Most churches making this kind of study are likely to see that they are doing less than they thought they were doing. Some of the areas discussed in the twenty-five chapters of the book are neglected or totally overlooked by many churches. The resources are available. Assistance in planning the educational ministry is available. What is needed is the active leadership of a few people (officials, teachers, parents—it does not matter where it starts) in crystallizing concern in a church and in helping the people to see the possibilities of Christian education.

It is hoped that this book will be useful to people who want to be doing whatever is needed to give their churches and the people an effective and wide-ranging educational ministry. Let us carry Christian education into the areas where the learning is!

V.E.F.

Contents

PART ONE

Persons Who Do the Learning

1 *Everybody*

Wants

to Know

Most people are asking profound questions. This fact is of tremendous importance to Christian education. People want to know the meaning of the dilemmas they face in everyday life. As one young man put it, "In a world that could be blown to bits before the sun sets, what is the point of life? If the world is not blown to bits, what assurance is there, when things change as rapidly as they do, that everything we think has value will not be obsolete in a little while anyway?"

"Who or what put us here in the first place? Why? Is there any purpose, sense, or meaning to existence? We are trying to beat everybody else to the moon but cannot solve simple (?) social problems here at home. If I am a member of a minority group, how long must I put up with second-class citizenship—I've had enough of it now!"

"If I am just graduating from high school, why should I sweat it out for four years in college to learn a job that may not be needed when I get through? If I do not go to college, what is there for me? They say that I'm through, finished, on the scrap heap at seventeen."

"If I have made it and have a good, safe job at forty-five, with a future, is it really mine, or is it a public trust? Why isn't it mine? I worked hard to get it—maybe harder than the person whose work did not pan out so well. Do I have any responsibility to him? What? Why? Who says so? Is there anyone bigger than my neighbor or my boss to whom I am responsible? If there is, why doesn't he make himself known, clearly, like a person who signs a contract with me? How can he hold me accountable? I have no agreement with him. Who is responsible to me? I didn't ask to be born. Who, other than Dad and Mom, in their mad innocence, put me into this crazy world, anyway? What, in the end, is to come of it, of any of us, when we get to the time when we can't take it with us? Then what?"

"I'd like to know some of the answers—maybe not all of them, but some of them."

People are not necessarily coming to the church with their questions. Some of them are, and feel that they are not getting much help. Isn't the church the answer house? Isn't the parson the one who is supposed to know the answers?

Others flounder, or find their way into coffee houses, taverns, clubs, gangs, recreation groups, or bull sessions and try on questions and answers for size. They may not be coming to the church, but the church can go to them and enter into the dilemmas with them. That is its job—to search for every person, join him in his quest for meaning, and witness to the gospel of Christ there in the midst of his situation.

Many people do come to the church, but that does not mean that they are a different kind of person, or have simpler questions and problems. No one's questions are simple, not even those of a little child. The responsibility of Christian educators is to recognize the profound seriousness of the mystery of life as it opens before young and old, day by day, and then enter into that mystery with people.

Because it faces real questions and problems with the people who are confronted by them, a church has the opportunity to work at a solid kind of Christian education.

Some people recognize the profound nature of the life in which time sweeps them along and in which they are searching for understanding. Others take only halting cognizance of the mystery of life, but can be drawn, sometimes with difficulty, into a serious approach to it. Most people, misled though they may have been, are searching for an interpretation of the puzzle they find themselves in, and for dependable guidelines to follow.

Some, frustrated by the defeat of their effort to achieve anything genuinely satisfying, jump to easy conclusions. They try to get what they want by any means—even taking it from someone else. Religion, they think, has nothing to do with the contemporary world. Since life does not make any sense, the way to live is to look for the kicks. Yet, underneath the crust of this pragmatic adjustment to circumstances is usually (always?) some willingness to look for other answers.

Some churches are more alert than others to their responsibility in such a world. A man about fifty years old visited the church of his youth and came away shocked. "My home church is still going along the same way it did nearly forty years ago," he reported, "as if nothing new had come to the face of the earth."

Many churches still offer stereotyped answers to questions no red-blooded person is asking any more. Or they act as if all the questions had been answered long ago. They miss the freshness, the terrible immediacy and urgency of the "whence do I come, whither do I go?" of the current world condition.

Other churches have come alive in the current scene. Bursting the seams of the conventional patterns of church programs, they have study and action groups all over the place. Volunteerism—dealing with everything from freedom marches, voter registration, Head Start, tutoring of potential dropouts, relocation of families, to re-training of adults—has captured the deep concern of former club addicts. Bible study groups have taken on a new meaning. Occupational groups meet to discuss the relevance of Christianity to given occupations.

Not all of the deep concern for involvement in the issues of life can be credited to churches. Much of it is a direct engagement of individuals and groups with the conditions about them. The struggle for freedom, at home and abroad, has jolted many people into a new sense of responsibility for their fellows. The threat of annihilation has made them aware of the relative unimportance and possible impermanence of the things for which they strive.

The war on poverty, thrust into dramatic immediacy by governmental concern and action, has made the plight of our neighbors visible and our responsibility in the matter inescapable. Issues rise up before us and refuse to lie down and be quiet.

What does all this mean to Christian education? It means that the situation is ripe for a solid approach to Christian education. The church must gear itself to look at life *with* people—life with all its tragedy, hopelessness, despair, and also opportunity. It must be with people in their need and as they come with the hot breath of the battle in their world, to probe for some rationale. It must recognize that there are no pat, easy answers, yet have faith that there are answers to be found—not just explanations, but deep meanings. The meanings are not always the accompaniment of success, health, and happiness. Many have little to do with these achievements.

Certainly, if we have any understanding of the dimensions and the character of the dilemmas that face us in the world, we must see that the work of the church is not accomplished in easy "Bible lessons." Whether adults, young people, or even (perhaps especially) children, the people we relate to are already in the midst of life with all its bafflement. Before we speak a word we must be with them and listen to them.

Who are they? What is staring them in the face? What are they asking of us and of each other? What, now, is their relationship to their creator? Are they aware of it?

The recognition of their relationship to God is the beginning of Christian education. We are on sacred ground. Let us not trample it with easy moralisms. If we approach people, alert to their present need and progression in their relationship to God, we can find our way into a solid, meaningful association with them as co-learners, searching for an understanding we all need and can share.

This meaningful association will not come without radical changes in our conventional, often stereotyped patterns of Christian education. Some of it will have to come as we develop comradeship with people in the midst of what is happening to them in the community. It will come as we help to strengthen the creative forces already at work in the community, playing a part in their lives and ours. It will come as we open to people activities within the church that help to meet their human needs.

2 Adults Cannot Quit Learning

The world is placing demands on people they have never had to meet before. It shows them that learning, changing attitudes, acquiring new understanding, achieving new skills, must go on throughout life. There is no longer a time when a person can say, "Now I have my education and I'm ready to take my place in life." Circumstances are changing so rapidly that we have to run intellectually, and keep on running, to stay even. There is a compulsion about this fact of modern life that cannot be ignored. Adults cannot stop learning if they want to be a significant part of the common life.

From the standpoint of securing and holding a job in which he may earn a living, a young person is required as never before to secure an education, then a re-education. There is still room for many people who want to take a chance with a single skill. There is no assurance, however, that many occupations will not be automated out of existence before a lifetime has passed. Occupational security lies only in one's having the kind of education that fits him for coping with rapid shifts from one major field to another, constantly learning the principles he needs to understand in the next field he may enter.

Yet, education is not just a matter of preparing to hold a position and earn a living. The world demands that each of us accept the obligation of responsible citizenship. The time is past when we can leave the running of the community, the nation, the United Nations, and the world to benevolent, father-figure politicians, while the rest of us take for granted the benefits of a speeded-up age.

Social structures we have taken for granted are breaking up under us. Many of them should break up. There is no need for panic or despair if all of us become involved intelligently in enhancing social change for the better. It may not be for the better. Who knows? It may be that things will become worse, much worse, before they become better. It is likely to happen unless there is a great uprising of intelligence, sanity, and devotion to the common good.

Issues emerge constantly that call upon us to learn to live in wholly new circumstances. They call for changes in attitudes that are hard to come by. They call for broader sympathies than most of us have acquired. These issues are real and they will not be diminished by wishful thinking.

What does it mean to be a responsible member of a community these days? What does it mean to have the privilege of taking an automobile onto the highway that is death row for thousands of people a year? We are living a new kind of life and we do not yet understand all that it means, not only to drivers, but to automobile makers, road makers, highway police, lawmakers, tavern owners, and all others involved.

What does it mean to be a citizen of voting age? Does the citizen's responsibility end with the polling booth? Is that where he can stop, leaving the rest to the winners? Or is there a citizenship responsibility that rests heavily on us during all the hours of the year?

What about the appalling cluttering of highways, streets, and parks with bottles, candy wrappers, newspapers, cigarette wrappers, and all the other junk we cannot seem to carry to the nearest litter basket? What about the tax cost of cleaning up the mess we should not make in the first place?

What about the graft, bribery, and immorality that corrupt basic principles of organized community life and will not be corrected until citizens accept their responsibility for vigilant involvement in that community life?

Such questions are insistent. The complicated rural and urban structures that have come into being will not stand if the majority of us abdicate our civic roles. Fulfilling those civic roles calls for continuing adult education throughout life.

For hundreds of years it was assumed that most of the people of the world would be poor, but that the poor did not need to be that way if they worked hard and thought big. These days of abundance, unemployment brought on by automation, and poverty aggravated

by the high cost of the necessities of life, call for a new way of thinking about the distribution of food, housing, clothing, and services.
A new conception of the interrelatedness of human beings is not
easy to arrive at or accept. Living reasonably in such an age requires
a degree of objectivity and sophistication that comes only with study,
discussion, and open-mindedness.

In this world of revolution and counterrevolution, one of the demands that is persistent and uncompromising is for freedom and
equality of opportunity, regardless of race, color, national background, religion, or any other barrier to equality. Easy assumptions
about differing native abilities have no place in the process of
achieving a new and acceptable social structure. The old order is
dead and anyone who wants to live in the new order has some learning to do and some changing to undergo—even the most alert and
educated of us. We cannot quit learning. The world will not let us.
We can even make a contribution to the change and help guide it
if we enter into our continuing adult education with open minds,
ready to look at the lessons of history and the facts of our day.

What are churches doing about this need for adults to keep on
learning? Some are doing very little about it. A few are even refus-
ing to recognize that there has been any change in our common life.
The minister of a "leading" church once said that the officials of
his church would not recognize a new idea if they met it coming
down the street.

Some churches have no organized adult education, or, at best,
only the most conventional and traditional. Others are making a
serious attempt to engage adults in the kind of study-and-action
groups in which changes of attitude and commitment can take place.

In examining its Christian education program to see if it is doing
all it needs to do, the first thing for a church to look at is its adult
education program. If it finds that no major changes have been
made in the adult program for five or ten years, the chances are
that a thorough overhauling is needed. The world has moved significantly during those years. Never again will it be as it was ten
years ago. If the adults in the church are not on fire with some fresh
ideas and are not on the edges of their chairs with concern about
the issues they are confronting, something needs to be done to jolt
them out of their complacency and bring them into the contemporary world.

Adults may start anywhere in their study, so long as they understand that it is not a stopping place. In one suburban church, adults started with small Bible study groups, but soon were engaged in various kinds of volunteer services to the deprived in certain urban areas.

In another church, adults started by studying the implications of Christianity for their occupations, but soon found that they could find no answers without studying the Bible and theology to learn what Christianity is about.

Adults in another church became concerned about their young people and their ignorance of the Bible, but soon discovered that they did not know much more than the young people. They began a systematic study of the Christian faith, its origins, and its meaning for today.

Some of the denominations that are launching new curriculum materials are publishing the new adult materials first, for they know that no Christian education can mean much that does not start with adults. So many improvements are being made in the materials for children and young people that adults have to be up-graded considerably in their comprehension of Christianity and their commitment to it to be able to communicate effectively with younger students.

One denominational leader reports that some adults frankly choose to be counted out of the venture into a more mature religious approach to life, and fall behind quickly in the development of their faith. She says, however, that those who risk the venture of engagement in the renewal of the church for its mission today generally come to a new appreciation of the meaning of men's relation to God and responsibility to him.

If a church has any conviction that secular references are not enough in seeking the resolution of the conflicts and needs of our day—that some comprehension of God's role in human history is required—then an immediate engagement of adults in study, discussion, and action is essential.

There is no lack of material for adult education. Nearly all denominations have published suitable materials. The main thing is for the adults to get started somewhere and follow through. Bible study, theology (Bible study that is anything but superficial gets us almost immediately into theology!), social problems, church history, biographies of great religious leaders, Christian art, hymns, the truly great religious plays (some of them contemporary), church architecture, anthems, missions, the struggles of the emerging nations, the church and governmental issues, international affairs, vocation, church unity—we can take hold at any of these points and soon find that one subject leads quickly to another. All aspects of life are interrelated.

One of the most important reasons for adults to keep on learning throughout life is that, whether they are aware of it or not, they are passing along to children and young people an impression of what they really think about life and man's relation to God. Adults may send their children to the church to learn about God, but they have done the most impressive teaching, for good or ill, before the children leave home.

For example, a first-grade child always came to church school in a bad mood and started pushing other children around and hitting them. The teacher was puzzled by his action until she learned that his mother always got the boy ready for church school in a flurry of excitement, rushing and scolding. He carried his resentment over into his behavior toward the other children.

Children are very alert to what adult behavior says to them about what is important in life. If adults take their religious faith lightly, this fact is communicated to their children and young people, no matter what they say about the importance of going to church school.

On the other hand, adults who are on fire with concern about dealing as Christians with the issues of life—and that means doing it as informed persons, constantly searching for enlightenment—provide a contagious setting for Christian education.

There is almost no time during the week at which churches have not held new and adventurous educational activities. There are forums on Sunday afternoon and any evening of the week, breakfast meetings, luncheon meetings, and supper meetings. There are large gatherings and small face-to-face discussion groups. The people of one church even held a weekly study and discussion program on a certain commuter train that carried many of its members to the city.

Among the most important things for a church to remember are the opportunities for Christian education that exist in many communities in colleges, YMCA and YWCA, seminaries, lay theological academies, and education centers. Many churches could help their members by calling attention to such opportunities and urging attendance.

As issues arise in a community they can become the focal points for educational efforts. People inevitably become involved in the issues, and ought to. Their churches can help them approach those issues in an informed manner by setting up educational sessions related to them. Churches can work together to bring into the discussion of critical issues leaders from within the community or from other communities, so that their members may become enlightened in their grasp of Christian responsibility.

The greatest opportunity for Christian education churches have ever faced lies immediately ahead. Adults, if they are to be a mature, significant part of the age, must keep on learning. Churches owe it to their adults to make this clear, and to open the way for adult study and action worthy of the name. They must provide opportunities in education that have some chance of helping adults to prepare for responsible living in an exciting, threatening, revolutionary time.

3 Children and Young People

in the

Main Stream

If Christian education is to mean anything to children and young people, it is essential that we recognize that from birth a child is in the main stream of life. All that he knows about the world is what he experiences from within his own life, in his associations with others. It is his life he is living. His relations with other persons and with the physical world expand rapidly, but he sees these always from his own position in relation to them. This is shown in the rapidity with which an infant develops a spirit of independence. Although he is utterly dependent on others for his care, in those areas in which he can operate under his own power he quickly develops his own point of view, because this is his life he is living.

The infant soon becomes aware of the responses of others to him. He is welcomed with love into the family, the community, the church, or he is met with hostility and rejection. He is greeted with a reasonable interpretation of the strange world about him, or he may be scolded repeatedly when he tries to discover what the world is like.

From the moment he was conceived he came into being in a relationship to God. However lacking in religious maturity his parents or others about him may be, the child is, in fact, in a functioning relationship with God. Experiences with other human beings may aid or hinder his coming into full consciousness of it, and may even cause him to rebel against God. Yet the relationship with God is not of our making. It is not a product of Christian education. All that Christian education can do is help the child become aware of the relationship that already exists, understand the nature of God, and live productively in cooperation with him.

When the child is brought home from the hospital he is in the main stream of life in that home. His parents and brothers and sisters may make it difficult for him to participate in the life of the family. They may resent his presence, may heap abuse on him, may eventually drive him from the home. Or they may welcome him with love and understanding. They may make available for his guidance their own experience, acquired under like circumstances.

When a child is brought (we hope not sent) to the church, he is in the main stream of the Christian fellowship. One of the reasons that many children and young people rebel against the church and leave it at an early age is that they are never allowed to feel that they are a part of the church and its life and work. They are given a room, or a corner of a room, to come to for instruction, but always for something to happen in the future, not now. That time seems never to arrive, and as young people they come to the conclusion that what they are being taught is irrelevant. So they leave.

If we want to see children and young people in their role in the church, we should not look first in their classrooms. We should see them in their relaxed, leisurely associations at church functions, such as dinners, corporate worship, picnics, coffee hour, family night, children's or young people's choir, the every-member canvass, social functions, and in the work of the church in the community and world.

The superintendent of a church school phoned the minister of education of another church that was noted for its Christian education program to arrange for a few new teachers to visit his church school. "We shall be glad to have them come," the minister replied, "but if you want them to see what is happening to our boys and girls they should come and stay a few days. Some of our classes attend congregational worship each Sunday, and your teachers should attend with them. They should visit the children's choir rehearsal, for it is an important part of Christian education. On Wednesdays the junior high young people come after school for a meeting with the church staff and stay for the Family Night Dinner. Then they should visit with some of the boys and girls about the ministry out in the community carried on by the classes. In watching a Sunday morning class your teachers will see only a small part of our Christian education program."

Although few churches have succeeded with distinction in opening their whole life to children and young people, the trend is in that direction. Children and young people are a vital part of the church in its whole life. To the extent to which a church opens its life to them it can make Christian education important to boys and girls.

Christian education does not have to be just a review of ancient events with indistinct interpretation of what they mean today. It can be a deliberation about this on-going Christian life in which the students are already deeply involved in church, home, and world. Christian education can be a process of self-discovery, as well as study of a great history. It can be a process of understanding self with all its wondrous possibilities, in association with other people engaged in similar discovery. It can be a process of coming to grips with the issues arising in the church and the world in which the students are inescapably involved.

Christian education can help persons, in association with each other, to explore their true existence in relation to God, as members of the church body and as sinners in need of repentance and forgiveness.

This does not mean that church school classes are secondary in importance. They may be part of the main stream of church life. Are they? Is Christian education, in the minds of the adults and families, part of the main stream? Frankly, are the adults engaged in Christian education as learners as well as teachers and leaders? Unless they are aware that they themselves need to learn, and unless they are engaged in studying the issues of life and the relation of the wisdom of the church to those issues, they are making Christian education a secondary part of the church. In that case it will not long be a primary concern for children and young people.

There is no substitute for a church all of whose members are engaged in study, worship, and mission. The emphasis on bringing children and young people into the larger life of the church as full participants is as it should be. In one church the minister was convinced that this should be done. The young people responded to the idea. Unfortunately, the minister had not taken the time to begin with the adults. Consequently, the young people found the adults going along on the easy assumption that they did their learning years ago when they were young and that they already knew all they needed to know for the decisions they had to make. The young people soon saw through them and decided they wanted none of such a church.

If adults truly want for their children and young people the best in Christian education, the most important thing for them to do is to get into the stream of Christian education themselves.

This does not mean that all adults have to be in classes on Sunday morning. It does not mean even that all the classes for children and young people must be on Sunday morning. A church that takes seriously the need for new information and understanding for all ages soon finds that one hour on Sunday morning is not enough, either for adults or children and young people. A church that is alive in its concern about the issues confronting its members and in its search for information that enables the members to live effectively, will find it necessary to have learning opportunities throughout the week. Such a church will find its boys and girls, as well as its adults, coming into the whole stream of church life—including study, worship, and ministry in the world.

When children and young people become critical of the church, as they will, we must let them enjoy the freedom to be critical from within the church, rather than as outsiders. If they are not allowed this freedom at an early age, and continuously, they will become critical as outsiders. We need the critical evaluations of the young. We need to know what the church looks like to them. They come with a fresh look. If we have attempted to cram Christianity down their intellectual throats as something new to them, to be "learned," to be accepted without question, we can be sure that there will be healthy criticism of it and of us. Furthermore, we shall deserve it. Criticize the church they will, even if we have welcomed them into full participation in its life. Under those circumstances, however, they can appraise the church as participating members of the fellowship. They can do it constructively, bringing fresh insight.

As we examine our Christian education program to see whether the church is moving forward in the light of the best we know, we need to ask ourselves how we regard children and young people. Do we think of them first as pupils whom we must teach about the Bible and church history? Or do we see them first as human beings coming into the center of our church and community life? Do we see Christian education as something we need as much as they in learning how to be responsible participants in the mission of the church in the world?

The problems children and young people face in trying to come into the main stream of church life is aggravated in many situations by the church building. The church school and other Christian education activities are held in a separate building or in a wing of the building remote from the places where adults gather. This seems to relegate children and young people to a position of secondary importance and makes it easy for adults to overlook them. Any church that has this kind of building needs to be extraordinarily careful to bridge this separation and make it as easy as possible for old and young to feel that they are in the same church and participants in the same world ministry.

How do we treat our children as they come into our church? Do we truly have two-way communication with them? Do they enjoy freedom to express their own deepest concerns, anxieties, hopes, and observations? Or are we expecting them to listen as we tell them what we think they need to know, without reference to what is happening to them deep down in their individual lives? These are questions each church needs to face honestly as it measures the effectiveness of its ministry with children and young people, and plans to improve it.

4 · That Is Where We Live

Although it is important that children and young people be encouraged to be a part of the main stream of the life of their church, it must be recognized that most of their lives are lived out in the world, not in the church as an institution. Most of their time is spent away from the church building—at home, on the street, on the playground, at school, in sports, on hikes, and (as they grow older) in part-time jobs. They are engaged in conflicts, contests, loves, and hurts, with pets, friends, family, and teachers. Gradually their society takes on form and organization, with rules, schemes, temptations, sex, personal habits, concepts, principles, career choice, and religious associations.

What have the church and Christian education to do with the young person in that kind of setting? It must do more than draw him out of the world to relate him to something that happened nearly 2,000 years ago. Out of the accumulated wisdom of the ages has the church something significant to say to him in the world in which most of his life is lived?

This question is not new. Christian education has always been directed toward helping persons live significantly in all associations of life. Yet, the world has come up and hit us in the face so hard in the second half of this century that we are beginning to be aware as we were not before of the extent to which we are first of all in and of the world. The church must speak to people in the world in which they find themselves. If the message of Christ is relevant now it must be communicated in the situations in which people have their being as God's creatures. God's love is current, not just historic, and must be witnessed to wherever people are. God forgives, heals, and redeems the penitent now, and this must be made clear now in the life of the church and the lives of its members.

Actually, recognition of each person's world makes Christian education more red-blooded and interesting than it seemed to be as a simple matter of indoctrination.

In examining its approach to Christian education, a church should give careful consideration and attention to the way it thinks of the people it teaches. The infant is born into the church, of course, as well as into the world. Yet he becomes aware of things outside the church long before he is conscious of the church as an institution. He comes to know a great deal about life long before he learns about the Bible and the church. He begins to live his life in the home and out in the neighborhood and community. He finds friends (and perhaps enemies) in that larger world, and he seeks some kind of meaning for his life in it. He may find in it some responsibilities to carry and a mission to perform that is worth giving his life to.

If the church is to be of any assistance to this child—and the young person and adult he becomes—it must be with him in his home, community, and world. It must "companion" him, share in his insights, show him the sources of courage, and in every way possible give him genuine evidence of understanding, acceptance, love, and forgiveness.

A person who attended church school faithfully all through his childhood and youth reports that it was an older brother who had more influence on him than all his church school teachers and ministers. This was because the brother was near enough to know what was happening when he was confronted by any new, strange problem. It was the brother who understood him, knew what to say to be of help, but did it calmly. It was the brother who could explain things that baffled him out in the world. Church school was never any problem to him. He went. He listened. Yet his attitudes were being shaped and his insights developed in his day-by-day experiences away from the church building. His brother was there to share his more mature experience.

This out-in-the-world setting of life is taken into consideration in the preparation of church school curriculum materials more today than it used to be. It is recognized more in the preparation of some materials than others. Yet, the leaders of a local church

are not likely to understand what this approach to Christian education means unless, even before turning to the curriculum materials,
they face up to the facts of the whole world in which their children
and young people live.

It is important to remember that all of us, leaders as well as
students, come to our Christian faith that way. We live out our
lives in the world with all of its good and evil, its rough-and-tumble
contests, its tremendous opportunities for discovery and achievement, its disappointments, successes, tragedies, and joys. Faced with
the hard reality of it, to whom do we turn for wisdom and understanding? Will it be to parents, teachers, the church? Will it be to
our peers around the corner or down the street? Will there be a
progression in the search for insight in books, journals, enlightened
conversation, and the arts? Or will the search be dissipated in a
downward scale of conclusions?

At times we are lost, and in desperation we call out for help.
This may not be in words. We may just rebel against the confusion
of it all and strike out blindly. Yet the striking itself is a call for
help. If someone happens to be around who cares and understands
(a parent, church school teacher, minister, or choir director, for
example), who can share the burden and listen, we may respond by
listening to what he has to share out of the wisdom of the ages.
He must be ready, however, to walk the lonely road with us, to
venture deeper into our world as we see it, if we, in turn, are to
walk with him.

The church speaks to people in their everyday associations or
it does not speak to them at all. We must understand that people
live, first and always, in the world of home, playground, school,
business, profession, social issues, civic responsibility, and international affairs, and that that is where the witness of the church to
God's presence in human affairs must be made.

This approach to Christian education opens to teachers and students alike an opportunity to look at the whole of life as having
religious significance. What students bring with them to church is,
therefore, of religious significance. The purpose of the teacher and
the resources he brings to the learning situation is to help the students see the religious dimension of "ordinary things," to see God
with them in the midst of life calling them to a vocation.

Where is the Christian's responsibility? Is it primarily in the church? We have been too prone to think that it was. Or is it in all the associations we have from day to day? Is God acting in the church only, or throughout the world? If God is acting in the whole world through the whole week then that is where the Christian's responsibility must lie primarily.

Where are the vital issues being fought out and wrestled with? It is out in that action that a Christian's responsibility lies. What has the church to say that will help a person in those associations through the week? A person's responsibilities are in relation to his fellow human beings wherever he finds them and relates to them.

One couple had no church background, but had taken seriously their responsibilities as citizens. Through observation they concluded that the church was doing more than any other agency to help find solutions to the world's problems. They started participating in the activities of a nearby church because they wanted to help it in its world ministry. They say that soon they found that the church had something they needed—a solid Christian faith and point of view, a gospel, as well as a mission in which they could share.

A teen-age girl who had attended church and church school regularly began to experience perplexities that were too baffling for her to handle alone. She had broken away from the church because she felt that what it taught was not relevant to the problems she and her friends faced. Nevertheless, whenever she had to talk things over with someone other than her parents it was to her minister she turned. She had confidence in him and felt that he was interested in her as a person, whatever her problems might be. He had entered into the lives of the young people beyond the formal program of the church. He attended some of their dramatic and athletic activities in the public school. He was never too busy to visit with them on the street.

One of the most effective "teachers" in one church never taught a church school class, but her influence on her own children and their playmates, boy friends, and girl friends was more important than that of any of their teachers. She was part of their lives throughout the week. Her understanding of their problems and decisions was always helpful.

This kind of Christian influence exists in every church, of course, but we do little to recognize, encourage, and strengthen it. Too often our "parent education" efforts are unsure and ineffective. A church becomes an important factor in the religious growth of its people when it helps adults recognize the value of their informal, day-to-day relations with children and young people, acknowledging these as the setting in which important work of the church is done.

Placing such relations in their proper perspective does not diminish the importance of the church school teacher. Rather, it emphasizes the importance of the through-the-week contacts of the church school teacher with his students and their families. One church, recognizing the importance of such contacts, provided each teacher with a team of parent associates to assist in arranging extra meetings of the teacher with his students in picnics, hikes, parties, and one-to-one associations.

Children and young people come to us busy with the "here and now" of life. That is where they live. What have we to say to them that has anything to do with, or makes any difference in, the way they respond to the things that happen to them? When they come to us they give us the opportunity to enter their lives, to be part of the solution to the problems they face, to help them find meaning and direction in the day-to-day realities of life.

This is a tremendously challenging opportunity. Are we facing up to it?

5 Go as Fast
as You Like

No two persons are alike and no two learn at the same pace. Also, no one person learns at the same pace in all subjects. In the past, many teachers have taught as if this were not so. We must discover, in Christian education, how to let each child, young person, or adult learn at his own maximum speed.

Learning at individual maximum speed depends largely on the teacher's (and parents') ability to understand each student, to discover his interests and abilities, and to open to him the resources for feeding his curiosity. A teacher who tries to get by with a minimum of effort and time given to his class will probably never discover his students' interests and abilities. He will miss the thrill that comes in knowing students individually and personally, and in helping each one strike out at his own pace.

Helping students to go at their own pace begins, therefore, with the teacher's developing his ability to teach at his maximum capacity. The supervisor, superintendent, and minister must come to know and understand each teacher, individually and in association with others. Only in this way can they help him see the importance of giving enough to his students to come to understand them. The teacher must develop enough curiosity about the student's future to give up some other interests in order to devote time to getting acquainted with him.

Planning a teaching approach and gathering resources can be exciting. Let us begin with the basic curriculum materials published by the denomination, all of them, those for parents and teachers as well as those for students—audio-visual materials, supplementary reading materials, hymn books, and pictures related to the curriculum books. Many age-group magazines for students carry recommendations of books and other magazines, and these should be used if a teacher is interested in helping every student move at his maximum speed.

Although some members of a class can move faster than others, the slow speed of one student does not necessarily indicate lack of ability. He may not be interested in the kind of reading material or activity proposed. In such cases, the teacher, through some other approach, may be able to discover a latent interest of the student. Also, some students require a more active approach to learning than others, and some are more able than others to think in abstract terms.

Some enjoy learning through drama; others are bored by it, or are timid. Some like to work with their hands and actually handle the materials; others prefer to use tools. Some students find creative art an enjoyable medium of expression; others enjoy working with ideas through reading and discussion.

One sixth-grade class decided to make a set of drawings on slides to illustrate the course. The original plan was for each student to make one slide and write the story to be used with it. Early in the quarter it became clear that some students were working much faster than others, and some were doing better art work than others. Before long, some students had completed several slides and were helping the slower learners with their work. Some found the writing of the stories easier than the art work, and they helped others with their stories.

Adults are equally varied in the way they approach learning. Some read widely; others read almost nothing, but are still interested in ideas. Art speaks to many and hardly at all to others. Some adults learn best when they can discuss and debate issues; others respond to ideas quietly, and mostly when they are presented by another person.

Such variations need to be taken into account. Why is it, for example, that the adult lecture class often has little appeal, and that the attendance sometimes levels off, no matter how much it is promoted? It is because a lecture class appeals to people who, although eager to acquire ideas, like to have them presented in well-organized form in a lecture. They may not care to read, do research, serve on study teams or panels, or even do much critical thinking about the ideas. On the other hand, if the church has no class that demands initiative, responsible participation, reading, discussion, or perhaps even occasional dramatization or role playing, then the people who learn best through these activities will not show up for the lecture group.

One church had held an adult class for years. The lectures were excellent. The class was the only one in the church with a paid teacher. Yet, attendance never reached more than about thirty-five. Then other adult groups were started and soon there were six, all thriving without diminishing the attendance of the lecture class. Each group appealed to people with different interests and gave room for individual initiative and learning.

Children and young people may come for a while to a class in which they are expected to sit quietly, but sooner or later they usually drift away. While they are sitting quietly, their minds are probably racing around in various active pursuits that have no relation to what the teacher is saying. In the end, their bodies follow their minds to where their genuine interests lie. This kind of child or young person is a challenge to the teacher who can discover him and his interests, and open to him learning activities in which he can engage wholeheartedly.

Many young people in high school have protested, "We have been coming to church school for fifteen years and we are still studying about Jesus—the same old stuff we learned in primary class." It is the same Jesus, but it does not have to be the same old stuff. There are many materials dealing with the meaning of Jesus' life and message in relation to the issues faced by high school people and every other age group, and by people of various professions, business occupations, and voluntary services.

These materials cannot all be compressed into the basic texts purchased from the denomination. Such texts are the basic curriculum guides, but there are many books and magazine articles published each year that can push the curriculum far beyond the beginning provided in the basic materials. Many of these are recommended in the basic guides. Every church, even a small one, needs a good library of them.

Branching out from the basic materials is one of the most important ways of stimulating the interest of all the students and of giving the rapid learners an opportunity to pursue their specific interests without breaking contact with their peers, as might be the case if they were promoted into an older class.

Small churches should not feel that individualized instruction is only for the large churches. It is especially important for the small church, which usually has more than one grade in a group. The older students in the group, and the rapid learners, may move out into supplementary areas of study and share what they learn with the slower students, thus helping with the teaching as well as increasing their own learning.

Branching out is not limited to reading extra materials. It can include extra activities, service projects, interviews, dramatization, creative writing, field trips, and preparation of equipment and materials to be used in the class.

Programed instruction may prove to be a very helpful means of letting individuals learn at their own speed in Christian education. Teaching machines and programed books are used extensively in some public schools and in industry. Some denominations are now developing them. Machines cannot take the place of teachers—they call for better-trained teachers—but they may come to be an important aid in Christian education.

In order to achieve more individualized instruction, one teacher supplemented his own observations with information about the progress of his students in other church activities, in public school, and in the community. He became acquainted with the director of the young people's choir, the Scoutmaster, and the leader of the young people's fellowship. He became acquainted with the parents, trying to sense the climate of each home and trying to learn from the parents how to encourage the initiative and imagination of the students. He learned about the capacities of some of his students from public school teachers he knew. He was interested not only in information about his problem cases but about the average and rapid learners as well. He learned about the young people's free-time activities in the community and found indications of their special interests and capacities.

A new appreciation of individual differences in learning ability has caused some public schools to adopt a more loosely-graded approach to teaching, with a mixing of ages in any one room. There is a trend toward larger rooms in which various learning activities are carried on, with relatively easier movement of students from one interest to another.

This is not a new idea to churches. In Scouting there is a mixing of younger and older members, coaching of younger Scouts by older boys and girls, maximum freedom to move as fast as the individual is inclined, and freedom (beyond the initial stages) in the selection of areas of interest.

Church choirs offer a similar opportunity for an individual to move at his own speed. Although the performance must be in concert, each member of the choir can learn as fast as possible through extra study, practice, and rehearsal. There is mixing of ages in children's and young people's choirs, with the more experienced members helping the less experienced.

Even if a church is not ready to move along completely with public schools in an unregimented approach to teaching, it can improve its Christian education by giving up lock-step procedures in which all students of an age are treated the same, and by offering enticing opportunities for supplementary learning and action.

This principle is important not only in work with the unusually talented student. It is important to encourage every student to learn at his maximum speed and in the way that is best for him.

A teacher needs to be alert to the possibility, however, that there may be in his class one or more students who have exceptional ability and who need special learning opportunities. Quite likely they need individual attention at some time other than in the regular class session. Some churches have found it wise to have a few qualified people available who are especially interested in working with the talented, to tutor and counsel students with outstanding ability. The students continue to be members of their groups, but they also have the friendship and guidance of the special teacher.

In encouraging all members of a group to learn at their maximum pace, a Christian education leader can (1) provide a wide range of interesting resources that invite individual students to special ventures in learning; (2) spend time with individuals to become acquainted with them and discover their unique interests and capacities; (3) discover what the individual brings with him from previous experiences; (4) involve each student in the larger life of the church and make him feel that he is part of all that the church does in its work and worship.

Each church must ask itself whether it is thinking big enough in its educational ministry. Is it helping each student learn at his maximum pace and find himself and his calling in life?

6 *Get to Know Them*

Superficiality is the chief enemy of Christian education. Teachers who do not take preparation and training seriously, parents who are unconcerned, pupils who will not do their homework, poor use of curriculum materials, and no use of supplementary materials are common problems. Under such conditions a teaching ministry is at best superficial, at worst meaningless.

There is another aspect of superficiality, however, that is not as easily identified, though equally disastrous. It is the failure of teachers to relate to students so that each can truly know the other, and so that the teacher may communicate with the student where he really is in his religious development. Even when a teacher makes the class program so interesting that the students respond with concentration and full participation, if the program is not related to the lives of the students it will have little or no meaning.

One upper-junior class formed a "reading club" for its members. To remain a member of the club a student had to read a designated chapter of the assigned book each week. One of the girls decided she would not read the material. Her grandmother urged her to do it. The girl said, "I don't understand the material or see any point to it." The grandmother said, "But you should read it anyway. Some day you will meet some problem, then you will remember the material and it will help you solve the problem." The girl replied, "I have a better idea than that—I'll put the book in my dresser drawer and when I run into the problem I'll get the book out and read it."

The girl had a point. The material may have had relevance for her right then, but she did not see it. Perhaps there was not the kind of understanding between her and her parents, grandparents, or teacher in which the point could be brought into focus.

Actually, the teacher of that girl's class had worked out a most interesting program. The students participated with enthusiasm and seemed to learn a great deal. However, there is another dimension to Christian education. Is the teacher listening to the students enough to know what lies "down under" the surface manifestations? Does the teacher know each student well enough to understand the personal and religious issues of his life?

"This stuff makes an interesting story, but you don't expect us to believe all this bunk, do you?" one junior-high student challenged. His teacher did not have to answer all the doubts expressed. Perhaps some of what he was "teaching" was bunk. In any case, it is healthy to bring the students' religious questions out into the open so that they can be examined calmly and with complete trust between students and teacher.

What does the study material have to do with John or Mary? Its relevance cannot be assumed. One of the great values of many of the newer curriculum materials lies in the fact that the planners and writers have tried to overcome the superficiality of teaching by dealing with the issues of life that actually are issues for the students. There is also an attempt to engage the teachers in thorough training and preparation. Once the teacher has a solid understanding of the content of the material, he can try to take hold wherever the student is in his religious pilgrimage and let the study of the material be an adventure in further growth for both student and teacher.

Paul Campbell had always seemed just like any other member of his high school church group. The sponsor of the group did not know him well, but by chance he learned that Paul was thinking of going into the ministry. There followed many conversations about the questions that Paul could not escape, that lay underneath all the things he did as a participant in his group's activities and discussions. Before this accidental discovery by the leader, Paul had begun to wonder whether anyone in the church was interested in him as a person. Many times he had wanted to talk with someone in whom he had confidence about what he should do with his life. He was considering giving his life to the church and its mission, but no one seemed interested enough to find out about it.

In one church young people coming home from college often sought out the sexton instead of the minister or the church school teacher. The sexton seemed to understand them better than anyone else in the church. There is nothing wrong with the church sexton being the best friend of the young people, and there is good reason for it. For one thing, sextons often serve the church longer than the minister and so get to know the young people better. But what an opportunity the other adults were missing—to know the young people on something more than a superficial level.

Many an adult has looked back on his childhood or youth and regretted that no adult in the church was sufficiently interested in him and certain questions he was wrestling with to help him make a decision he failed to make. If only an adult had shown an interest in him and accepted him as worth listening to, the decision might have been made. It could have been the church school teacher, in the classroom early and ready to listen, or lingering after the session to chat quietly, or meeting him on the street and inviting him to have a coke at the drugstore, or calling at his home to share his hobbies and listen at the same time.

Getting to know each member of a group more than superficially takes time. But time is not the big problem. The major requirement is an attitude on the part of the leader toward his students, and an understanding of what, after all, is most important in the teaching ministry of the church.

The teacher must have, and be willing to share, a great body of information about the Bible, Christian history and biography, Christian art, and Christian tradition. This information must be organized so that it can be studied in logical sequence. The church should strive for a commitment on the part of each student and for his participation in the mission of the church in the world. Nevertheless, the information must be regarded as a resource, a well of knowledge and inspiration, with which to deal with the essential needs of each member of the group.

A man who had been active in the church school for over thirty years was talking with a young woman about the church school teachers who had influenced her during her childhood. To the man's surprise the young woman had only vague recollections about one teacher the older man thought had been unusually efficient. She remembered several others clearly and with great appreciation.

She could not remember much about what they had taught, but she remembered that those teachers had taken the time to know her personally and to listen when she needed help with a personal problem. They got down under the surface to where she lived.

The primary objective of the teacher must be to understand where each student is in his unique individual development. Where is the student at a given time in his relationship with God? Is he having any problem in understanding that he has such a personal relationship? Is he aware that God has a purpose for him? What are the student's struggles in understanding and meeting the expectations of his peers? Are there conflicts at home? How is he getting along at school? If he is behaving rebelliously, what is he trying to say through his rebellion? Does he feel rejected and alone? Is he insecure and struggling for status with his peers? Does he see any sense in life? What are his attitudes about the great social issues of his time? Are his attitudes objective, or do they say more about him than about the issues?

Are both the teacher and the student aware that most of their experiences, educational and otherwise, take place away from the church building? Their religious life takes on shape and meaning, positively or negatively, in associations the institutional church has had little or no part in shaping. Yet the church can be a factor in those situations. Teachers and students should recognize that God's action takes place throughout the life of the community, and that they can be a positive force wherever the issues of life are being faced and decisions made.

Beneath the superficialities, there may be all kinds of concerns, uneasy attitudes, and individual problems that arise from the issues that confront the person. If the church goes along casually trying to package religious information and Christian faith for its members, in easy Sunday morning doses, it will slide right over the major issues that shape the student's thinking and response to life. It will do a superficial and meaningless kind of education.

If, on the other hand, the people engaged in Christian education take the time to be understanding friends of their students—children, young people, and adults—the door to significant Christian nurture may be opened. If they take the time to listen to what the students are saying, verbally and nonverbally, there will come many opportunities for the teachers to say things that are relevant and meaningful to the student out of the great body of accumulated Christian wisdom. It is what is beneath the superficialities that counts for the student, and must, therefore, be of prime concern to the teacher.

7 On the Move

The fact that people are on the move is often thought of as a serious handicap to the church. "I'm preaching to a procession." "We get our church school leaders trained, then they leave us, moving to some other community." "Few of our boys and girls stay with us from nursery through high school." These are but a few of the complaints. One church reports that it has more than one hundred per cent turnover in its constituency every year.

There is no denying that a shifting population brings problems, not only to the institutions serving the people, but to the people themselves. Some people never put their roots down long enough in any one community to be a responsible part of it. To children and young people the breaking of ties with friends can be heart-rending, and the community of their new home seems strange for a while.

Even people who do not move from one community to another often travel so extensively on weekends that they get to church and church school only occasionally. It is difficult for a student to get much out of what is being studied if he is present only for a few sessions during a quarter.

Some churches that are severely affected by population movement and weekend travel have tried to find at least partial solutions to the problem in various ways. Some of them hold a church school session during the week, on Saturday, or some weekday in the late afternoon or evening, as well as on Sunday morning. Some of these churches have had a remarkable attendance of families for weekday sessions. Other churches have worked out an orientation program in which new families moving into the community are drawn quickly into the fellowship and helped to catch up with the church school curriculum, choirs, Scouts, and other groups. There is room for more experimentation along these lines, and churches should be alert to the needs of families moving into and out of the community and those who are away on weekends.

There are, however, potential advantages that come from being on the move, and these should not be overlooked. A church can help people broaden their outlook and enrich their education through their travel and frequent change of residence. A church can help its people to become good travelers who come to know a country, not just move through it. It can help them learn how to make friendships quickly in a new community and to approach a new home or vacation spot with an inquiring mind.

Many churches have members who have returned from trips report on them. A church can carry on, as part of its educational program, a travel information seminar or bureau to acquaint families with interesting places to visit along the path of a projected trip. There are art museums, historic churches, mission centers, colleges, the ministry in national parks, national and area denominational and interdenominational offices, work with different ethnic groups, the United Nations, areas where social issues are especially crucial, national church camps and assemblies, locations of the Boy Scout Jamboree and Girl Scout Roundup, church furniture factories, church window studios, new churches of special interest, church retirement homes, church hospitals and orphanages, and other places that many travelers pass by without knowing they are there. Some families are willing to visit some of these places in their travels and give reports to groups to which their members belong.

A few churches make a point of recognizing those of its members who are about to travel abroad. They stress the point that the travelers will be representing their church and country abroad, even though unofficially. The churches keep in touch with the travelers while they are away and welcome them home when they return.

The teacher of a church school class that was made up of members from many different places found the group fascinating to work with. During discussions the members shared experiences from other communities and states, and in one case another country.

A church can make the most of the mobility of its people by

learning where its members come from and giving each family an opportunity to contribute its unique experiences to the fellowship. Even visitors present for only one Sunday can enrich the lives of church members. In one large urban center, for example, there is a church in which hardly a Sunday goes by without at least one visitor from abroad, and sometimes several. There is a coffee hour after church, which provides an opportunity for people to meet and converse with these guests. The guests share not only the interesting experiences that come from travel, but insights about social conditions in various areas as well. This is helpful to all.

One church school group corresponded with a member who had moved away and thus helped him to feel that he was remembered with affection, and consequently to find his way into the new community. He, in turn, sent back interesting reports about his new friends that made the group feel a part of his new ventures. There was some visiting back and forth, and people in one community began to feel acquainted with those in the other. Horizons were widened through these experiences.

A new member of a group, coming from some other community, state, or country and leaving friends behind, should feel the warmth of Christian friendship in his new church and church school. This is a moment of testing for him. Will the group open its doors to him and welcome him into full participating membership, or will he find a cold attitude toward strangers? His experience on coming into the group can confirm his impression that Christians are friendly, concerned people. If, on the other hand, he meets with a cold reception this may turn him away from the church, possibly forever.

The teacher of a church school class should find out from the new member what curriculum materials he has been studying in the church from which he came. They may be different from those used in the school to which he has come. The student may need help in becoming acquainted with the materials that are new to him. Even if the materials are the same, one class may have moved faster than the other. One of the classes may have used more enrichment materials and activities, such as supplementary reading, audio-visuals, field trips, art projects, and interviews. Careful attention from the teacher in introducing a new student to the curriculum materials and making the student's family acquainted with the activities of his class will help the student feel at home and ready to make a contribution from his experience in his former church and community.

This orientation should include making the new student acquainted with the church librarian and the books in the library that may be especially interesting for reading at home. It should include making him acquainted with the church school superintendent, the minister, and the choir director. The church's resources should be available to the new student, as well as all students. The orientation of a new student can be an experience of value to all the members of a group, making them aware of the personal, literary, musical, dramatic, artistic, and other resources with which each member can be strengthened for his role in the world.

Every church should arrange frequently for new members of various ages to be taken into the church sanctuary and given an interpretation of whatever symbolism is to be found in its design, its architecture, and its windows. A brief review of the history of the church will help the new members feel that it is their church too.

Rapid turnover in a church makes it important that Christian education groups be small enough so that members can come to know each other, and that there be a leader for each five to eight students. Some church school groups in which new members are received frequently make a practice of having a name tag for each member. If the pupils are too young to read, the leaders should know the individuals well enough to speak to them by name; they should speak the names clearly so that the children can learn the names of their new friends. One parent discovered that her child did not know the name of his teacher, although he had been in the class with that teacher nearly a year.

In another situation a teacher of a high school group discovered in the middle of the year that few of the students knew his name and many of them did not know each other. Such incidents occur more frequently than we think, and remind us how urgent it is to become acquainted with our students. An atmosphere of strangeness, thoughtlessness, and unconcern is not conducive to learning.

Many teachers find it difficult to call in the home of a new pupil soon after his arrival, but such a call is valuable and helps a new family feel that it is a part of the community.

A great number of churches are near colleges and universities where students from abroad are studying. Many of these students, unfortunately, are never welcomed into homes and churches in the host communities. Some churches, however, make a point of welcoming students from abroad and introducing them to church families. They find the lives of both the members and the visitors enriched by the friendships formed.

There are dangers in population mobility that cannot be ignored. Sometimes it makes people feel detached, rootless, anonymous, without close friends. The church, then, should be constantly alert to make the newcomers feel welcome as responsible, participating members of the church and community. Informal periods in church school and youth groups, in which group participants become acquainted with a new member and learn of his former activities, help break the ice for the new member and open doors for new friendships to form.

Recognition of the dangers inherent in a rapidly moving population must not be allowed to blind us to the advantages. Travel can be a broadening experience. Living in several different areas of a country can enrich one's experience. A person who has lived in a rural area, in a city, in a coastal community, in a mountainous region, or with people of other races, cultures, or nationalities and has become acquainted with the institutions and customs of those areas, may be much more interesting to know than a person who has lived all his life in one neighborhood without traveling. The traveler may contribute more to the Christian education program.

Instead of being frustrated over the disadvantages of mobility, we should accentuate the benefits. Recognizing mobility as one of the facts of modern life, let us make the most of it. While a family that is likely to move is with us, we should learn from its members and help them to have such rich experiences that they will be ready to move when the time comes and will know how to participate responsibly in their new church and community. In this way we can help make mobility educationally valuable to all.

8 A New Day
for
the Handicapped

Churches should get much of the credit for awakening men to the worth of every individual in the sight of God. But churches, along with other institutions and the community in general, still seriously neglect people who deviate from normal. The physically handicapped, the mentally retarded, the emotionally disturbed, and persons in custody are tragically overlooked. Although much public interest in persons with special needs has been aroused recently, and although progress in ministering to them is being made, many local churches still do not provide adequately for them. When a church examines its Christian education program it should make sure that persons with special needs are given their rightful place in its fellowship and ministry.

Exceptionalness is a relative thing. All people deviate from normal in some respect. Also, persons who have serious handicaps are usually normal in other ways if they are given the opportunity. Handicapped persons have a normal need for acceptance, affection, understanding, forgiveness, hope, and a chance to be useful and to achieve.

Even if all the students in a church school fall within the average group, there will be a wide range of intelligence and capacity among them. Even those within a close range do not all learn in the same way or at the same rate. Some of them have a serious need for learning in certain areas in which others of the group have already matured. Trying to teach all the children or young people in a group as if they have exactly the same needs and abilities is a serious mistake.

One of the problems in working with exceptional persons is that of preventing the differences they have from dominating their lives and damaging their development. The great challenge to Christian education is in helping each person, whatever his exceptional condition, to live to his fullest capacities, whether normal or deviant. The capacities of exceptional persons are far greater than most people understand, once help, counsel, and education are provided in accordance with their needs.

The physically handicapped

Let us first consider the church's relation to the physically handicapped. It has been estimated that one out of seven men of working age is disabled by crippling or chronic illness, and one out of sixteen of the total population. This means that there are few congregations that have no physically handicapped persons in the parish. Some are in institutions, some must stay at home. Many others simply retreat from social contacts because they cannot climb stairs, or do not want to be embarrassed. Still others, of course, do participate in church activities.

In one small city a man who became concerned about the ministry to handicapped persons found that there was not a single church building in the city that could be entered without climbing stairs. Any crippled person would have to be given assistance or be deprived of attending church meetings. This situation is almost typical, but better provision is being made in many new buildings, and many churches with old buildings are now installing ramps.

Persons with serious physical impairment are likely to find themselves handicapped as much by public misunderstanding as by the physical condition. This extra handicap can and ought to be removed. It is difficult for a disabled person to accept his handicap until he feels himself accepted, wanted, respected, and loved. This kind of acceptance a church can extend.

Many physically handicapped persons have great potentiality. One blind person types eighty words a minute on an electric typewriter and writes books. A cerebral-palsied man became a successful artist, holding his brush between his teeth. Another is a social worker and an author of important articles. A man without arms became a minister and denominational executive. A young man, blind from infancy, went through a university then went on to earn a master's degree. Many blind people have become successful ministers, authors, and executives.

Churches can do much to help the people of a community understand the possibilities of the physically handicapped, and to see to it that everything possible is done to help them develop their capacities, so that they may have their rightful place in society.

When it is at all possible, people with physical handicaps should be included in regular groups. They may need help in getting to the church, but be able to participate once they are present.

Because of the increasing awareness of the need to include crippled persons in the church's program, more attention is now being given to making church buildings usable by them. Guidance in this matter is available from the National Society for Crippled Children and Adults, 2023 West Ogden Avenue, Chicago, Illinois 60612. The Society gives information about how to plan for wheel chair ramps, stairs with the right kind of rails, warning bars for the blind at doors that open onto stairs or drops, toilet accommodations for people in wheel chairs, stair risers that provide maximum safety, and other important features needed in both new and old buildings.

It may be harder for a crippled person or his family to achieve faith in a loving God than it is for one who has full health and use of his body. Nevertheless, he needs that faith to help him face his handicap, accept it, and live to his full capacities.

The mentally retarded

It is estimated that approximately two per cent of the population are severely retarded. Twice that many are sufficiently retarded to need special attention in Christian education.

Not much was done for the retarded before 1800. In 1842 Horace Mann advocated special schools for them. In 1848 such a school was started in Massachusetts. In the 1930's parents began working together to secure for their retarded children the training due them. Not until 1950 was the National Association for Retarded Children started.

Surprising as it may seem, one of the problems in working with the retarded is that of identification, especially in the case of the slightly retarded. Educational retardation is sometimes mistaken for mental retardation. The educationally retarded may be normal mentally. Nevertheless, many of them, thought to be mentally retarded, have been confined to institutions and have lived there for years before their true ability was discovered. How many of them have died there without their normal intelligence being discovered will never be known.

On the other hand, many persons who are mentally retarded have made their way in society, earning a livelihood in routine jobs, without their retardation being recognized.

One of the thrilling discoveries of recent years is that many retarded persons have undreamed of capacities, when they are given the kind of education or training that makes the most of those capacities.

If retarded persons are to develop their capacities fully, their families must have around them an understanding community, a church that helps them deal intelligently with their special needs, and the help of the church and community agencies in securing the training and education the laws guarantee to all.

A church has a special responsibility for ministering to families of retarded persons, helping them learn what they have a right to expect of the community, the schools, and the agencies. It can help parents find fellowship with other parents of retarded children. Many retarded persons can be included in the fellowship and activities of a church. In general, they respond well to affection and understanding.

In most communities, when special classes and social groups are needed for the severely retarded, churches find it best to work together. For example, in one city a special class is held in one church, but is open to children from all the churches. In another the Council of Churches has provided leadership for developing several such classes in different parts of the city to serve all retarded children, some groups for younger children and others for older ones. In still another city churches have provided an evening youth fellowship for retarded young people who come from all over the urban area.

The emotionally disturbed

Work with emotionally disturbed persons presents some especially difficult problems. Emotional disturbance is hard for a lay person to identify with certainty or deal with. It can be mistaken easily for mental retardation. Often the treatment received in a church group, or even at home, aggravates the disturbance because the leader or parent is uninformed or may not have full emotional health himself. On the other hand, mature, understanding volunteer Christian education workers have been able, in many instances, to relieve the pressures causing or aggravating emotional disturbance.

Except in severe cases it is best to keep an emotionally disturbed person in his peer group and to help him find emotional health in normal associations with people his own age. One young man had deep emotional problems, probably because of a rigid, dominating mother. He was understood and accepted by his church young people's group, in which he found his chief sense of security. His disturbance continued into adult years, but he looks back to his associations in the young people's group as the most meaningful of his life.

Often the individual needs associations with his adult leader outside the regular class or group activities, and may even need help from a psychologist, physician, counselor, or psychiatrist.

When we recognize that emotional disturbance is likely to be brought on either by a health problem or by the pressures of an unhealthy social situation in home or community, we can see the urgency of the church's responsibility for bringing understanding, love, and intelligent guidance to disturbed persons. At the very least a church is responsible for providing mature Christian education leaders, and conditions which encourage self-confidence, freedom of expression, opportunity for achievement, and normal social relations. Furthermore, the church is responsible for providing the kind of leadership education that will help its Christian education workers recognize emotional disturbance, know the basic things to do about it, and understand when it is necessary to seek professional help.

The church is supposed to specialize in bringing the messages that are most needed by emotionally disturbed persons—the assurance of the love and forgiveness of God; an understanding of the meaning of life and the high calling to self-forgetting service; the declaration of the worth of all persons in the sight of God; the needlessness of fear and panic; and the ground of hope.

In its whole life and in its specialized Christian education groups, a church has the opportunity to make this ministry a reality for persons disturbed by pressures they do not know how to cope with. One must, of course, go beyond the symptoms and deal with the causes of the disturbance, however manifold and obscure they may be.

We must not, however, fail to do all we can to help *all* people achieve emotional and mental health. It is a health all of us need and perhaps none of us has in full measure. All suffer occasionally from emotional stress, even injury. Therefore, we can join together in the search for self-understanding, in discerning the pressures upon us, and in perceiving the vocation in life to which each of us is called.

Persons in institutions and in custody

Many churches have an opportunity for a special ministry to persons in institutions and in custody. Working together through their Council of Churches, the churches of an eastern state have rendered a particularly significant service to persons in institutions over a period of many years.

Some churches have worked with people in jails. Other churches and church schools have taken a special interest in the families of persons in jail or prison—families that often are forgotten or shunned. Such a ministry is important, not only for the help it gives to the persons in institutions and their families, but also for what it does to those in the church who remember that God loves all persons and that all of us share in making his love known.

A church or its Christian Education Board or Commission can make a study of its own population area to discover whether there are jails, juvenile homes, crippled children's homes or hospitals, residential schools for the blind or deaf, or any other institutions whose residents ought to be included in its ministry of education and fellowship.

One community found that some of the children in a crippled children's home could come to church school and other meetings if the churches could provide transportation, which they did.

In another community a single church took the initiative in working with persons in jail.

In still another the children made presents for men in a nearby prison to give to their children as Christmas presents. The prisoners and their families showed great appreciation, and the children of the church gained a new understanding of the problems these people face.

Who is responsible?

One may wonder who should initiate a ministry to any of these persons with special needs. It can be anybody. Logically, the cooperative ventures should be initiated by the council of churches or ministerial association. Indeed, the supervision of the effort should probably be in the hands of the council of churches or some cooperative organization created especially for the task. But actually, the initiation of such a move often comes from an individual or small group of concerned people, perhaps parents. Let no one concerned think that it is some other person's responsibility to take the first step.

In a local church the Board of Christian Education or the committee on social concerns might be thought of as the responsible group. The first step, however, must often be taken by the people with the most concern and the most vision of what needs to be done. Particularly in a local church no one should feel that it is some other person's responsibility to arouse the congregation to action.

One of the most important things to do first is to train the leaders. Much of this training is the same kind needed for work with any group of children, young people, or adults. Work with exceptional persons, more than other kinds of ministry, requires in its leaders the ability to listen as well as talk, to relate patiently and lovingly with the members of a group, to keep long-range objectives in mind at all times, and to recognize the special needs of individuals.

Some of the specialized education that leaders of exceptional persons need can be provided within a local church. However, in most cases it is best for churches to work together in setting up the training program, through the council of churches if there is one, or by special arrangement if there is no council. In most communities leaders of agencies, doctors, educators, and parents will help the church provide the training.

No one procedure for working with exceptional persons can or need be proposed. Different communities have worked out a great variety of approaches, according to the needs and resources of each. A new awareness of the church's responsibility for ministering to all people, however normal or specialized their needs may be, has brought to many churches the challenge of a broad, humane, loving, and theologically and biblically sound educational ministry that they could not have conceived of otherwise.

Some churches have rendered a much-appreciated service to people temporarily or permanently confined by illness or injury by taking Christian education to them in their homes. A striking example of this occurred when members of a group of young people called on a young man they had heard about who was discouraged and making a slow recovery from illness. His attitude improved almost at once and his recovery became much more rapid and finally complete.

In other instances classes have kept fellow members up to date in their Christian education studies during a recovery period. Each need must be dealt with individually, in terms of the specific situation, but the possibilities of extending Christian education to those confined must not be overlooked.

There are several points at which a church should give attention to persons with special needs:

1. Both laymen and clergy should become acquainted with the best literature about these persons. It is constantly increasing and improving.

2. They should become acquainted with the various local, state, and national agencies. Porter Sargent Publisher, Boston, Massachusetts, publishes a *Directory for Exceptional Children* that lists educational and training facilities.

3. Churches are in a unique position to interpret to the public

the special needs of these people and to interpret to the families involved the needs of their children and the facilities available.

4. Churches must rethink their ministry of education, worship, and fellowship to make room for more attention to the individual needs of *all* people, and to get beneath the surface in dealing with them.

9 *No Talent*

to Spare

Among those most seriously neglected by the church and other institutions are the academically talented or gifted. It is hard for most of us to comprehend the waste of talent that takes place because of this neglect.

It has been generally assumed that the highly talented would look out for themselves; but it does not work that way. The talented often become discouraged in public and religious education systems that focus on the average person. Some, unable to understand their predicament, rebel, drop out of church school, or even turn to anti-social behavior.

With the talented, as with the retarded, one of the problems is that of identifying them. Many people of high intellectual and creative ability are not recognized as such, and spend their lives in occupations that demand only a small part of their potential.

Contrary to popular notions, the genius is not typically a small, stooped person wearing thick glasses. As a group the gifted are above average in size, health, looks, and social ease. They commonly have a large and precise vocabulary, unusual curiosity, coordination, self-reliance, social adjustment, and interest in reading, music, and art. They come from homes with little educational background as well as from privileged homes. However, a lack of educational encouragement from the parents makes it more difficult both to identify the individual and to work with him.

Even from a selfish point of view a church should give attention to this group. Some talented people can find their way into church occupations and render outstanding service as ministers, directors of religious education, teachers in church-related colleges, denominational and church council executives, and missionary doctors, teachers, and agriculturalists. Also, persons with unusual capacities offer great possibilities in lay leadership.

Service to the church, however, should be a minor consideration in a church's motivation in ministry to gifted persons. Its goal is to help all people achieve their maximum development as creatures of God. None of us can fathom the mysteries of personality or predict the capacity of anyone, whether his endowments be small or large. But, of all the risks of history, the most productive is the giving of energy and imagination in order to encourage people to follow their highest dreams.

One of the common methods of uncovering talent is to provide adequate educational opportunity by enriching the curriculum with extra reading, learning activities, and stimulating associations. This is not enough, for the highly talented need a curriculum designed for them. Nevertheless, much can be done through enrichment, which, unfortunately, many churches do not attempt to provide.

If talented children and young people are to be discovered, there must be an opportunity in the Christian education program for the leaders to come to know the students individually. Leaders and students must work together in the learning venture, and the students should contribute their ideas, suggest activities, and accept responsibility in the group. Consequently, the program has to be relaxed and permissive enough to allow for companionship among the students and between the students and leaders. There should be more than one hour a week in which associations between leaders and students can develop. Some churches devote as much as three hours on Sunday for Christian education; others hold extra sessions during the week. Committee meetings, conferences with individual students, field trips, library sessions, and special project meetings provide extra opportunities for the leaders to come to understand their students from the inside out.

One church school leader who took the time to get to know and understand each of her students had an outstanding record of motivating her students to learn. She was always at the church early on Sunday morning, and many of her students responded eagerly by coming early to converse and work with her. She formed committees of the children that met with her during the week, and, as the students responded to these extra opportunities, she brought together those who seemed to have unusual interests and abilities, hoping that they would stimulate each other, which they did. They shared hobbies, reading interests, and responsibilities and developed a sense of companionship in their learning experiences. Many of her students went on to remarkable achievements in business and the professions and in volunteer service. They looked back on their year with this one church school teacher, who took the time to be their companion and encourage them, as the year that made the big difference in their lives.

Although there must be an opportunity for individuals to express their ideas, a talkative person is not necessarily the one with the most advanced ideas. He may instead lack self-assurance and a sense of worth and be trying to talk his way into recognition.

Nor is the one who is most aggressive with responsibilities necessarily the best equipped for leadership. He may be seeking recognition, or an opportunity to assert himself in a role that has been denied him in other associations.

It is essential that the Christian education program be open ended. There must be opportunities to read, to enter into conversations outside the organized program, to engage in extra activities, and to become associated with adults in the church other than the group leaders. There must be opportunities to form companionships with other students, to engage in services to the church and through the church, and in every way to move at one's own speed in Christian education.

When opportunities such as these become available for all the students in a group, it may become apparent that some of the students are intellectually superior and need the special attention of someone more skilled. The leaders can then seek specialized counsel.

Any church can carry out these suggestions if the leaders are sufficiently concerned to give extra time. Gifted people are likely to appear in any church, and leaders should be on the lookout for them. Since few of us are skilled in recognizing them, the best way to be sure of giving them the educational opportunities they need is to encourage all students to make the most of their potential.

We do not educate anybody, be his intelligence low, medium, or high, simply by talking to him, by telling him. We should seek the student's help in tailoring Christian education to his own needs and interests. This takes time and sympathetic interest. But there is no other way to make Christian education meaningful to any child or young person. When we reach for the best in every student, we are likely to find it in the gifted as well as the average or the handicapped.

The central importance of this matter to any church that is re-examining its educational ministry is revealed in the experience of a church in the Midwest. One of the leaders of the church school discovered that there were two boys, one in a junior group and one in junior high, who, according to their public school records, were unusually talented. The church school teachers were given guidance in their associations with these two boys, and, as they came to understand the two students, they and other leaders in the church school discovered some basic educational principles. As a result a quiet transformation in the entire church school took place. Much more emphasis was placed on understanding every student and on helping him achieve according to his maximum capacity. The educational program became less rigid. Students entered into the program with more zest and developed friendships with persons in the church other than their teachers. The religious experience of all the students and teachers was enriched as a result of the concern for the two gifted boys. These boys, in turn, found the educational atmosphere of the church stimulating. They responded to the op-portunities provided and fed back into their groups ideas and enthusiasm that were contagious.

In summary, there are several things a church can do to help discover and educate the intellectually endowed:

1. The church is in a good position to alert its community to the need for better opportunities for the talented.

2. Although a church probably does not have all the resources for final identification of superior intelligence and creative ability, it has a remarkable opportunity to contribute to identification, and may be the first to discover hidden talent.

3. A church has a primary responsibility for interpreting to parents the possibilities of their talented child or young person.

4. A church must work in close cooperation with other agencies for its gifted students.

5. Most churches could give much more attention to individual differences, so that each person has the opportunity to develop his capacities fully. The church may have to rethink its present program of Christian education, and take a hard and honest look at itself to be sure that it is providing the kind of atmosphere and program in which intellectual capacities can unfold.

10 *Premium*

on

Creativity

Much has been made in recent years of creativity or creative activities in Christian education. This is all to the good, except that many teachers understand little about creativity and its importance in the learning process. At its worst, creative activity is busy-work that keeps the student occupied but does little or nothing to whet his curiosity or allow him individual experimentation. Even in the better programs it is often creative only within a very narrow range, giving the learner only a limited experience of developing something new out of his own skills and knowledge.

Acquiring basic information and skills is necessary for creative learning. Many of the skills a child or young person needs to experiment creatively, such as reading, spelling, mathematics, and drawing, are acquired in public school. They need not be learned again in church school, but they can be used there. Some of the knowledge acquired in public school should be supplemented in church school. Geography, for example, can be supplemented with information about the Holy Land and surrounding countries, about areas rich in Christian history, music, or art, and about areas of missionary activity at home and abroad. Historical information can be filled in with facts of special religious importance. Public school social studies should be supplemented with information about the church's concerns. In the church school we should take into account what the student has already learned in public school, in his home, in Scouting, YMCA, YWCA, clubs, and in private lessons in painting, music, dancing, and other arts and crafts.

Individuals vary widely in the skills and information they have.

Consequently, some are ready to move quickly into a creative use of them, but others need more instruction before they can venture far. Pushing a student too fast in the development of new and original experiences can bring discouragement.

This does not mean that a student cannot begin any creative experimentation until he has acquired a certain grade of skills and information. Training and creativity should go hand in hand in the learner's growth. We should recognize that the creative venture can take place only when a student, led by his curiosity and imagination, tries to accomplish something that for him is new and exciting.

One of the weak spots in Christian education has been our failure to help students understand how to use the knowledge and skills we teach them to meet their own needs and interests. In general, we have failed to make clear even that they have any relevance to real interests and concerns.

In some of the newer curriculum materials an attempt has been made to correct this situation and to open the way for the learners to keep the issues of their lives in focus, even while studying something that happened two thousand or more years ago.

We should not think of creativity as something of which only the intellectually superior are capable. No matter how intelligent a student is, no matter how old, we must let him start where he is and move forward experimentally at his own pace. We must help him be aware of the skills and information he already has as resources with which to move into new ventures.

The validity of this educational principle can be verified by watching children and young people when they are free to do whatever they want. One will sit and read because he has skill in reading and has already developed a thirst for the kind of information he knows can be found in books and magazines. One child and his pals used their knowledge and skills to try to make a rocket. One boy built a clubhouse, using lumber from an old building his uncle let him tear down. Another made a boat. One girl was always inventing new games. Others dressed up in make-believe clothes and worked out a dramatization. Something whets the curiosity and imagination of each in a certain direction.

If given the freedom, children will use whatever information and skills they possess to pursue new ventures on the most interesting frontier of their experience. Some will make more of a contribution to the venture than others, but all are likely to enter into the undertaking and learn in the process of carrying it out.

Not much is known about what makes creative experimentation come about, but we do know that it is most likely to occur when certain learning opportunities have been established, when an attitude of expectancy prevails, and when the student is allowed a high degree of independence within the general objectives of the program.

For example, in most public schools children learn at an early age to perform simple research and investigation, and they are encouraged to do independent reading in search of information. They may be encouraged to interview people who are sources of information, or they may write to agencies and bureaus for information. These research skills can be used in Christian education to bring together facts needed in the course of study.

Many church school teachers and leaders find their students responding with enthusiasm and imagination to the opportunity to use their skill in group or individual investigation. Adding new information to the knowledge already acquired is likely to result in new insight and understanding.

A group of high school students in one church who were about to enter college interviewed adults of various occupations. They asked about the requirements of the occupations, personal satisfactions, range of income, and other matters of interest. Six of the people who had been interviewed were then invited to speak and answer questions at meetings of the group. Some of the students indicated later that the candor of the people interviewed and the information they shared contributed substantially to their choice of an occupation.

An important part of the motivation for learning comes when a student can see how the knowledge he is acquiring is related to possible future experiences. For example, one group wanted to dramatize a Bible story. The members were excited about the dramatic possibilities. They already knew the general thread of the story because it had been told to them and they had read about it in the text. They discovered, however, that they knew little about how the people dressed, furnished their homes, cooked their meals, or even what kinds of foods they ate. Immediately a motivation was established for further study in order to learn these things. Then the group had to present this information realistically in the drama, and a certain amount of creativity was needed to make the drama as true-to-fact as possible. Out of this effort came a new understanding of the Bible people.

Creative experience is not a thing that can be controlled or predicted with certainty. We may not even be able to recognize it for sure when it comes, and it will not always happen at the same time for all members of a group. It will seldom happen at all if we use teaching methods that thwart individual initiative or if we expect all members of a group to conform to a rigid, predetermined session plan.

In most church nursery groups there is a great deal of room for individual experimentation and achievement. Many nursery groups provide several centers of activity in which individuals may spend their time as they choose. There may be a housekeeping center, a painting area, game tables, a building-block area, and a music corner.

The tendency in Christian education, too often, has been to restrict the areas of individual initiative more and more from the kindergarten on through the grades and even into the young people's groups, whereas the exact opposite ought to be the case. If it is valid to let a nursery child exercise initiative in selecting his area of activity, the older child or young person who has increasing capacities for experimentation, research, invention, and problem solving, should be given more of an opportunity to use them. He has wider and deeper areas of interest he should be encouraged to pursue. Presumably he has more skills and information that are relevant to the critical issues of life through which he is trying to find his way. He should have the freedom to employ them.

The critical issues of life are religious (and theological) in nature, as well as social, economic, and personal. The insights gained in studying the Bible, church history, Christian art, music, and biography are relevant to them. The student must have the opportunity to discover this relevance and to bring new and old knowledge together in an effort to figure out solutions.

There is no easy way to provide for the creative experience in learning, but it will not happen without the teacher trying. Once the teacher recognizes that he can learn from his students as well as they from him, the way is open to establishing with them a companionship in learning. This companionship will put a premium on individual initiative and systematic progression from old to new information. This kind of learning venture allows for creativity.

We should remember that learning is most exciting when it pushes us out to the frontiers of our curiosity. We should always try to make learning creative, and the learner should be at the steering wheel with his foot on the accelerator, rather than in the back seat. We may not know at what moment the student crosses the threshold of creativity, but he will probably never do it unless we put a premium on creativity, investigation, and experimentation and provide the permissive, expectant atmosphere in which creative learning can take place.

11   *Time on*

Our Hands

For industrially advanced nations leisure has become an important phenomenon. The production of boats, skis, bowling alleys, billiard tables, skates, sports clothing, camp equipment, and a thousand other items for use in leisure time has given rise to new growth industries. Churches, which have depended in their activities almost entirely on the free time of their people, have had to make radical adjustments to compete for that time. Some churches hold services and church school during the week as well as on Sunday, to accommodate families that want to spend their weekends boating, camping, golfing, swimming, picnicking, or traveling. Many find that fewer and fewer members are willing to commit themselves to regular teaching in Sunday church school, ushering, or singing in a choir.

The redistribution of time has been going on slowly for a long time. The ten-hour workday and the six-day week went out for most people many years ago. Recently, the tempo of change has picked up as a result of unionization, automation, and the exploitation of leisure by recreation industries.

There is some doubt about how highly many persons value free time. Many people sell their increased free time in a second occupation, sometimes a full-time one. They want more money for a second car, a bigger house, more home conveniences, more travel, college for their young people, to pay off debts, to support relatives, or for more insurance. There are many things they want more than they want time on their hands, or even time with their families.

There is one thing the church must remember if it is to take a responsible attitude toward leisure. As less and less time is required from most people for producing the necessities and luxuries of life, there is increased need for these people to spend their free time in volunteer services. The increased population, and the urbanization of popular tastes have created social needs unknown a generation or two ago.

In addition to the educational work done by professional teachers, there are preschool children to be helped by volunteers in church nurseries and Head Start programs, poor learners and dropouts to be tutored, illiterate adults to be taught, continued adult learning to be carried on, and many kinds of recreational activities for all ages to be conducted. The need for volunteer service in hospitals is increasing. If political activity is to be kept out of the hands of corrupt machines more people must give time to it, from local committees all the way up to national concerns. The provision of local, state, and national parks and recreation areas for use during leisure time depends on the concern and action of volunteers as well as public agencies. The need for volunteer services that must come from the gift of part of the new leisure time continues to grow.

These developments come in the face of the fact that most people have had little education in the use of free time. Churches and schools have done little to help people live fully during free time. Although churches talk much about stewardship of time, energy, and resources, they have done little to help their people develop a theology of leisure, or an understanding of how to pursue gracious, relaxed enjoyment of fellowship, music, literature, drama, the arts, and travel. They have done little to help people see how to balance their leisure-time pleasures with volunteer service in the interest of the whole community. It is time that churches and other agencies take seriously the responsibility for this education.

There are, basically, three ways of using free time: for fun, for self-improvement, and for service.

Free time for fun

Free time for pleasure and exercise is a basic right of every person. It is important to the health of body and mind. Through its wise use the range of one's interests can be expanded, the body can be freed from fatigue, and a deeper meaning of life can be experienced.

Many people have never learned the best ways to enjoy free time. They are utterly bored when nothing is required of them. They are often the ones who have the most free time, and they fritter it away in meaningless activity, or worse, in pursuits that are destructive both to themselves and their communities.

Churches, schools, and clubs must face up to their responsibility for offering to their own members and to the people of the community an opportunity to learn how to enjoy free time on many levels of activity, and to participate in organizing leisure-time ventures.

One church offers courses of study in drama, painting, bell-ringing, nature study, languages, and other fields in which the members have shown interest.

Another church offers courses to young people in sewing and cooking, crafts, painting, photography, first aid, music, drama, and other such activities.

Free time for self-improvement

Enrollment in adult education courses is said to equal approximately half the adult population and more than the enrollment of children and young people in public schools. This does not mean that half of the adults are taking these courses, since many of them are enrolled in several schools and are counted two, three, or more times. On the other hand, many adults linger in intellectual stagnation at a time when the world needs everywhere the brain power of alert, growing citizens.

Many adults keep themselves physically fit through regular exercise. Others grow fat and lazy, less and less able to respond to emergencies, less and less competent to make the most of the opportunities that confront them. They deteriorate in health and appearance. The physical fitness of children and young people is so shockingly low that schools and other agencies have been enlisted in physical-fitness programs. Churches have for the most part turned away from any responsibility for the physical health of their people except insofar as they have supported hospitals and clinics.

The churches have also exerted only a limited effort in increasing the intellectual vitality of the people apart from their own religious, social, and civic concerns. A few churches have conducted weekday nurseries, and more recently some have started Head Start programs and the tutoring of slow learners and drop-outs. Some are providing literacy classes and a wide range of hobby and language classes.

One church has made a distinguished contribution to the self-improvement of the children and young people of its community by offering dress-making and cooking classes, through which the students may lift the level of their present home life and become better home-makers of tomorrow. The dress-making students give a fashion show each year, wearing the aprons, dresses, and slacks they have made. Many of the students continue the study for several years, and their progress from making simple aprons to attractive dresses is clearly recognizable and remarkable.

There is increasing ferment across the world, with new nations leaping into the twentieth century and older nations into the age of automation and atomic power. There is consequently a critical need for talent and leadership in every sphere of life. Churches and other educational institutions must educate for the fullest possible use of each person's capacities. There is little free time to waste if the people of the world are to respond with dignity and integrity to the demands of the new day.

Leisure for service

There is not enough money for us to buy our way into tomorrow and the tremendous opportunities it promises; it will be what we make it, and much of the making must come through the contribution of free time in volunteer service and leadership. Those who *have* cannot move far into tomorrow without taking the *have-nots* along with them one way or another. The have-nots will walk upright into a better day if those who have knowledge, culture, and faith will share these through volunteer leadership. If this does not happen, the haves must carry the burden of the deprived in staggering taxes.

The handicapped also require volunteer service. With an adequate ministry by churches, many handicapped persons can participate in the life of the community much more fully than they can now.

One church has significantly assisted movements within its community by acting as a recruiting agent for securing volunteer workers. The fact that members of that church are giving various kinds of volunteer service is of value within the Christian education program, in making the members aware of their responsibility for movements toward social improvement.

Service and improvement
can be fun

In many instances all three benefits of the use of free time can be realized within a single activity. It is fun to swim, but the fun of swimming can be increased by teaching another to swim. Reading is fun for many people, but its enjoyment can be increased by teaching others, slow learners or immigrants, for example. Self-improvement through reading or research need not be dull—it can be tremendous fun, and it can become a part of an individual's service to the community if it equips him to tutor a potential leader who is about to drop out of school. A project undertaken as a service often leads to enjoyable friendships and a delightful sense of participation in an important accomplishment for the community—downright fun.

Motivation for use of free time

One of the important contributions churches can make to the valuable use of leisure is in the field of motivation. This does not mean that all the church needs to do is talk about the responsibility of other agencies in education for the use of leisure. Churches have to back up their speech with action, demonstrating how education for the use of free time can be carried on.

Among the most important and effective demonstrations are those made cooperatively through city mission societies that carry on far-reaching programs, especially for the underprivileged. In some instances it is a year-round program, conducted basically in the city, but extended during the summer into a camping program.

Education in the use of free time should be started at an early age and continued throughout life. The way to learn how to use free time after retirement, for example, is to learn how to use it in childhood, youth, and early adulthood.

To be sure that it is carrying on the kind of educational ministry it ought to provide, a church will want to evaluate the contribution it is making to its community in education for the use of free time. The need for the church's contribution is urgent.

12 *Learning*

in

Small Groups

Churches organize children, young people, and adults into small groups for much of their program activities, yet many of those groups are sleeping giants, potentially powerful but relatively ineffectual. Many of them are leader-dominated, pressed into serving the objectives of the leaders without much regard for the needs or wishes of the members. They are used for the manipulation of people rather than for giving them maximum release and participation.

Since small groups can be effective, both in learning and in action, churches should re-examine the ways they are working with them to be sure that the possibilities are not being dissipated. The mere fact that people are organized into groups does not guarantee that those groups will operate democratically, creatively, or redemptively. It does not mean that the members will immediately find acceptance and trust or will participate responsibly. It is possible for a church to have all of its active members enrolled in small groups without any of the groups functioning effectively as a channel of learning or action.

What are some of the principles by which a church can awaken its small groups? What is the unique function that can be performed by small learning-and-action groups?

Members of many small groups are learning to do a new kind of *listening*. Listening is not new in the church. It is as old as the church itself. Yet much of the listening in Christian education has been one-way. A leader stands up and talks to a group and the members listen. In a discussion each member may be more interested in hearing his own comments than in listening to the ideas of others.

Each waits impatiently for the first opening to cut in with his comment and does not hear what the others are saying. One of the principles that has come to be emphasized in small-group behavior is that each member shall listen to others and try to hear what each is saying—verbally and nonverbally.

If there is a stated leader, he most of all must listen to the members of the group and try to hear what each is saying, or what he is crying out for silently, unable to articulate his need. In order to give members of the group an opportunity to express themselves meaningfully a leader should say less, time his contributions so that they are relevant and so that the members are ready to hear what he is saying, and let as many of the ideas as possible come from members of the group. He should encourage members to listen to each other so that they hear and understand what is said. This kind of sharing cannot be planned in minute detail, like an address or a lesson, but it may open the way for learning more than a lecture will.

This kind of listening—opening one's mind to hear what another is saying—leads to *understanding and acceptance* of people for what they are and are becoming. It leads to an understanding of their needs, frustrations, ambitions, and shortcomings. When members of a group try to listen to one of their number, to hear and accept what he is saying or doing as worthy of their understanding, their attention is turned away from themselves in concern for the other. When the one listened to joins others in an attempt to hear, understand, and accept still another member, he loses whatever self-centeredness he may have had.

When the members of a group give of themselves in this way, a situation is created in which each individual has the freedom to be himself and express himself without manipulation or domination by others. Members can disagree with each other without fear of rejection or scorn. Each member is thus encouraged to make his maximum contribution to the group, knowing that others will not sit in judgment over what he says or does, but will receive it with understanding and appreciation.

When each member feels that he is accepted, trusted, and honored, he is relieved of the need to defend himself. This enables him to listen to others and to accept them for what they are. A young person who had never been in such a group moved to a new community. He became a member of a group that respected and accepted him, but it was some time before he could believe what was happening and trust the other members. He was on the defensive —quietly, but nonetheless with his guard up. He reports that when he became convinced that his contributions were treated with respect he found a joyous release in being, for the first time, part of an accepting, honoring fellowship. A new life began for him.

Out of these experiences of mutuality there can come *Christian love* that is founded on genuine respect and concern for one another. It is a nonsentimental love in which the Christian recognition of the supreme worth of a person takes on concrete meaning: "This person is a creature of God's making and is worthy of my concern and love, even if at times he seems obnoxious. I must understand not only what this person is, but why he is what he is, and what he is trying, by God's Grace, to become. Rather than stand in his way, thwarting his attempts to discover himself, I must let myself be an aid to his becoming."

In this permissive situation, a group can arrive at an understanding about *group goals*. Determining the goals and purposes of a group is not an easy task, especially since these should change from time to time, moving forward as one set of objectives is achieved. It is easy for a leader to set up in his mind a set of objectives, but if these are not the goals of the group the leader will find himself manipulating the members in an effort to achieve his own purposes. Also, one or more members of the group may attempt to manipulate the other members toward their purposes. It is only through patience and complete frankness on the part of the members that an agreement about goals can be reached that will form the basis for responsible participation by all.

This does not mean that it is possible for all members to participate with equal responsibility at all times. Circumstances may make this impossible. In one group an individual, in his anxious struggle to find himself and the meaning of his being, became estranged from the other members. The members of the group sensed what was happening and recognized the opportunity to become a redemptive fellowship. They reached out quietly to the estranged member, to extend love in the midst of his tribulation and help him find his way back into a responsible relationship with the group. For a while it seemed as if they would fail, but one member in particular was able to communicate with him and represent the genuine affection of other members.

From time to time a group will want to *review its progress* and evaluate its accomplishments. It may need to bring its activities to an end to make way for more important associations. On the other hand, the time may have come when the group should divide into several new units, each of which, in turn, will set about finding an identity and determining its goals. A group may find that it has failed to achieve its purpose, and needs to backtrack to make a new start, with a clearer understanding of what it is trying to accomplish.

Any group of young people or adults in a church is under an obligation to re-examine itself from time to time, to be sure that in the economy of mind, energy, and emotion there is a need for its existence and that it is serving that need well.

In recent years many adults in churches have developed an interest in small study-and-action groups. They meet at various times during the week; the newer ones are more inclined to meet on weekday evenings.

Many of these new groups meet for Bible study, but to study the Bible, not just hear about it. Some groups that started with Bible study found themselves impelled to move out into action, serving human need in their own or nearby communities.

Some groups concentrate on theology, Christian faith, the relevance and meaning of Christianity in various occupations, or fellowship. Whatever interest a group starts with, its concern is likely to spread to other areas.

If a church already has leader-dominated groups with established practices they do not want to change, this does not have to block the development of more creative groups. Moved by a sincere desire to probe deeply into subject matter and human relations, a small group of people in one church gathered without even the help of the minister or director of Christian education. It met on a week night so as not to disturb the established groups. Its venture was so rewarding that soon other small groups were formed, in which some of the members of the established groups participated. Each group chose its own subject matter. Some groups met at first primarily for intimate fellowship and decided on goals and programs after they were formed. Several of them soon became action as well as study groups.

It is not just adults who need the intimate associations and shared decision-making of a small group. Children need them too, and the logical place to have them is in their church school classes.

It is the lack of these self-determining associations in the home and church plus, often, the threat of deprivation, rejection, and insecurity, that drives children and young people to form antisocial gangs. These groups offer their members acceptance, security against danger, recognition, and an opportunity for courageous (perhaps reckless) action. The peer group in the neighborhood may provide the only association in which the child or young person finds any sense of meaning or security. The group demands intense loyalty from him. Everyone outside the group becomes an enemy and threatens the permanence, perhaps the existence, of the group. Therefore the group comes to exert a tremendous influence and control over the individual member.

This is not to suggest that every peer group outside of the church is antisocial. Sometimes more is learned in voluntary peer groups, at least about social relations, than in many church school classes. Learning takes place in these groups because real issues are faced, questions are tested on an apparently valid scale of values, responsibility is accepted, and decisions that have been made are lived with.

Participation in a church group can help a person become a constructive member of a voluntary group in the community if it gives him the opportunity to deal with real rather than hypothetical issues and to learn how to draw on dependable resources in meeting those issues, all in an atmosphere of acceptance, respect, and love, where there is freedom to make mistakes.

What is even more important, the needs of the children and young people are being met. The members are working out together the answers to the questions that inevitably arise in the process of growing up. They are trying on ideas for size (including Christian ideas) not just listening to them as abstract dogmas.

One of the most important developments in Christian education has been the recognition that God is already at work in the lives of children and young people before the teacher comes into the picture. Moved by the creative power of God in their lives the students are already trying to find their way, individually and in relation to each other. They may be seriously misguided in their search for meaning and self-expression, and many of their actions may be rebellious and antagonistic. But as long as we recognize that God is a part of their search and struggle we are compelled to recognize their integrity. Demanding that the members give attention only to what the leader is saying accomplishes little. We can influence the human venture in which the students are involved only by becoming a part of the venture with them.

It may be hard to recognize the importance of joining the students in their venture when the teacher and pupils are given a body of curriculum materials to master. The teacher may feel that the only way to succeed in his leadership role is to dominate the group in a regimented program. The most successful teachers, however, are those who assume that the students will find the material interesting once they see that it is related to their search for answers to basic questions about life: how it began, why we are here, the point of it all, and what will come of it.

If we listen to children and young people we soon find that they are asking profound questions. They may not be able to articulate them in polished language, but the questions are there. If we do not let them ask them of us they will ask them of each other, but if the group is permissive the members do not need to wait until the meeting is over and they are by themselves. If the members feel that the adult leader accepts and understands them, the important questions start flowing.

One high school group worked out its own programs for both Sunday morning and evening, with one set of officers for both sessions. Its leaders were sponsors and counselors rather than teachers. When the officers met in a home to do the planning, word would get around and the whole group would come. In the permissive atmosphere of the meeting questions that were of genuine concern to the young people were proposed and these became the basis for building a program. Progress was evaluated and goals for the months ahead were developed.

In another group one new member, recognizing the genuineness of his acceptance and of the trust established in the group, revealed that when he took friends home with him his father offered them alcoholic beverages, which was embarrassing because none of his friends drank. He did not know quite how to handle the situation and brought his friends home less and less. Out of the discussion that followed, in which he discovered that two others in the group had faced similar situations, he decided to talk with his father and try to help him see that the young people preferred soft drinks. For this young man this was an important step in which he was aided by his comrades.

The better Christian education curriculum materials are so designed that they help the leader and group bring out into the open the questions that need facing. The materials provide a biblical and historical perspective in which these important questions can be discussed more profitably than with only a short-range view.

For a group to be competent in dealing with the real issues of life, the members must be able to relate to each other freely in an atmosphere that encourages their listening to the point of understanding and accepting each other. The members must be able to share in planning the group's objectives and program and in making decisions. From this kind of participation the members will come to trust each other and to have confidence in their ability to face any question, problem, or task together. It is when those conditions prevail that learning can take place most profitably, and the learning can move on into decision and action.

Not all the activities in a church need to be undertaken in small groups. There are many occasions (corporate worship, church dinners, forums, social programs, and other meetings) when large numbers, or the entire congregation, will come together. These large gatherings are more meaningful if the members, old and young, have had an opportunity in small groups to come to know and understand each other, to develop concern and affection for each other, and to work together in the church's mission.

Furthermore, a church that has learned how to release its small groups in creative listening, study, decision, and action, gains from the experience some ideas for enhancing its participation in community groups. Some of these groups may be antisocial in their behavior, but God is as active in working with them as he is with groups in the church. He needs us to join him there, understanding the people he loves and working with them. Our purpose must be only secondarily to win them to the church; primarily it should be to help them find themselves by God's Grace wherever they are. Doing this is one of the church's great responsibilities and opportunities.

The church group can be a laboratory in human relations, in which we work through difficult situations with our comrades, developing the competence we need to meet our responsibilities as citizens. These difficult situations should be true, not imaginary. There are enough live situations and issues to be faced, at every age level, that we need not trump up fictitious ones. Issues in the community are crying for the leadership of people who have come to understand the hidden dimensions of human relations that Christian insight can reveal.

13 Learning and Teaching in Teams

The team of teachers and other Christian education leaders is most important for developing good group relations. If Christian learning is to take place anywhere in the church it must come first in the Christian education team. The teachers themselves must be students.

In recent years many churches have organized their children, and sometimes their young people, into groups of from twelve to twenty-five members, with each group under the leadership of a team of three to six adults. One of the adults usually acts as head teacher, or lead teacher. Each adult carries certain specific responsibilities, but at times all of them work together with the students, particularly in such activities as art work, drama, crafts, creative writing, puppetry, play, learning new songs, or several of these at the same time in different subgroups.

The team of teachers usually meets during the week for planning. Some teams meet every week; others try to plan for several weeks or a month at one time. The leaders find that in their companionship, in planning and working together, there is strength. Working alone often becomes discouraging. In the team arrangement the special skills of the various members can be used to full capacity. A team member who is weak in one area, such as storytelling, can make other contributions. Teams often find that meeting once a month is not enough. Meeting every week gives them so much more competence in their leadership, and so much more enjoyment in working together, that they are willing to give the extra time to the meetings.

When teachers work in teams each comes to see each pupil

through the eyes of the other teachers, and this usually helps a teacher to understand and accept the student.

There is another dimension to team teaching, however, that is often overlooked. Members of the team should study together and probe the deeper meanings of life in order to strengthen their own Christian faith as adults. Their teaching should be out of an overflow of religious experience that has deep personal significance. Members of the team should share their own concerns and insights, helping each other to grow in faith and commitment. Then they will come to their students with a growing appreciation of what the Christian faith and mission are about. They will come with a better understanding of what it is that they need to do in their relations with the students. Also, they expose their own growing edges to their students.

As this team association develops, its members may gain enough confidence in each other to share some problem that is weighing heavily on one of them. In a spirit of acceptance and love, the other members may be able to help their friend find a solution, or at least gain courage to face the problem, perhaps creatively. Such an experience of going through tribulation together helps them, in turn, to understand their students, and to listen to the unverbalized concerns that may be troubling individual students.

In one junior church school group a girl had been causing a good deal of disturbance and was annoying other members of the class. The leaders had shown impatience with her. Then they began to increase their own study and devotion, along with their planning. One of the teachers, who had some difficulty in entering completely into the team associations, finally broke into tears and revealed a personal problem that had her seriously worried. Realizing that she had exposed her concern in anxiety, but also in a newly acquired trust, the other members of the team attempted, in strict confidence, to share wisdom and courage in any way that would be helpful.

As a result of this experience, one of the teachers was moved to make an attempt to understand the pupil who was annoying the others. She thought that possibly the girl was acting, similarly, out of personal anxiety. She made it a point to converse leisurely with the girl. She mentioned occasionally some personal concern of her own. "I used to be very timid around other people, and it took me a long time to get over it. I guess I really was afraid of other people.

Maybe I still am at times. Yet I know that I should not be—that people really want to know and love a person. Often I've been surprised at how ready neighbors and friends are to give help whenever I need it. I guess life is quite wonderful when we let it be."

There were other self-revelations by the teacher. Often it was about something the teacher enjoyed. In response the troubled girl relaxed, became interested in the conversations, and even exchanged observations with the teacher.

One day the girl said to the teacher, "I've been worried a lot about my mom and dad. They used to scrap a lot. Often it was about me. Then I began to wonder if maybe I was causing it—doing things on purpose to get them started. It was you who started me thinking about it that way. You know, I've tried to be more agreeable at home lately. Believe it or not, my parents don't argue like they used to. Home is beginning to be a pleasant place to be. Your being nice to me helped me to see through myself. Thank you for it."

This experience helped the team of leaders to see the importance of their own religious growth and of relating themselves to the members of the class as friends. They were able to listen, unafraid to share their own concerns with the students, and to share with them in the venture of learning.

Some churches have succeeded in developing this team feeling beyond any one group of teachers so that it includes the entire Christian education staff.

Such a team feeling can be cultivated. Teachers' meetings can be planned so that the entire staff finds enrichment in them. Confronting important questions and discussing them again and again informally can lead to a deepening of Christian faith and commitment.

Every Christian education staff should meet at least once a month, and the meeting time should not be consumed by trivia. If the meeting is planned for the enrichment and education of the team members it will send the teachers away with profound joy and a sense of sharing an important task with others. Many teachers come to feel that their best friends are the other teachers, and that it is to them that they can turn in time of trouble or special need.

In one church the Christian education workers developed this fine team spirit so well that they became known all over their state and in surrounding states for their outstanding feeling of comradeship in the teaching ministry. Having this rich experience of Christian fellowship and concern, the teachers taught out of their own first-hand knowledge of Christianity and what it means, rather than just out of textbooks. The real person of the teacher and the real person of the student were exposed to each other. Communication took place that was more than theoretical.

This team spirit can reach beyond what is often thought of as the church school staff. In one church a crew of people with special skills gathered around the church school staff. These people came to feel that they were also part of the team. Some had skills in drama, music, rhythmic movement, puppetry, and crafts. Others could contribute information about a particular unit of study. One man was able to discuss with young people questions about Christian vocation and various occupations. Another was an unusually well-informed Bible student. Still another had a wide range of interests to share, including music. Among other accomplishments he had sung professionally in a Hebrew Temple and knew a great deal about the Jewish faith and practices.

In one church a woman with an understanding of children's problems agreed to join a teaching team in order to give most of her attention to one child who was having difficulty relating to the group. Working patiently with him over a period of several months she was able to help him feel his way through some of his personal anxieties and become a participating member of the group. The adult's relations with the other members of the teaching team sustained her in this special assignment so that she was able to be a creative companion to the child.

In another church teachers in each department of the church school had working with them a group of parents who were responsible for helping them in any way possible. Although these parents never became an intimate part of the teachers' study program, they did enter into the team spirit. They might have been drawn deeper into the teachers' adventures if the teachers had thought to invite them, and they probably would have welcomed the opportunity.

It is important that the members of the Christian Education Board or Commission share in the team associations of the teaching staff they supervise. Often the members of the Board think that determining policy is their only responsibility. Sometimes, however, policies are established that make the teachers' work more difficult rather than facilitating and strengthening it. This occurs because the members of the Board are not sufficiently sensitive to the needs of the teaching staff. When they participate extensively in the fellowship, study, and planning of the teachers, their decisions become less arbitrary and easier to live with.

The Christian Education Board or Commission should include among its responsibilities the development of meaningful team relations among the teaching staff, and should lead the way. The Board can provide the circumstances, opportunities, and occasions that help to build associations among the teaching staff that will bring about a recognition of need, and mutuality in the search for answers to it.

Regular meetings of the teaching staff, coaching in the use of resources and procedures, planning sessions, occasional social gatherings of teachers and their families, and conferences between each teacher and his supervisor, help to build fellowship and to develop the kind of commitment to the task that contributes to team feeling.

Most important in the development of a solid team approach to Christian education is a local church that is in truth a learning church. When the whole church is caught up in many kinds of learning ventures, it creates an atmosphere of respect for continued learning that compels the Christian education staff to match the church's spirit with its own. As teachers come to feel that the task is too big to be carried out haphazardly they will face their needs together in small teams that permit them to share their own concerns and probe for answers to the questions both they and their students face. If they have faced these questions sincerely as teachers, searching for answers, they can be ready to expose themselves to their students as searchers, inviting them to join in the search.

14 *Art for*

Our Sake

There is so much of wonder and mystery, joy and tragedy, beauty and ugliness, amazing order and wanton destruction in life that snap judgments about the meaning of it all are certain to be more of error than of wisdom. So much of life is almost beyond comprehension that the only fitting posture for human beings is one of alertness, expectancy, and searching. This is a difficult posture for many of us to assume and maintain, because we crave easy answers, simple interpretations, and abundant rewards for small efforts.

We find it easy to live with squares and straight lines but difficult to feel at home with curves, sweeping distances, rhythms, tones, change, infinite variation of color, and deepening shadows. Even when, at last, we turn from the low road to the high road we want sophistication to come at a small cost.

But it is only when we understand that life is made up of an unending complexity of experiences and insights and that it changes from moment to moment that we begin to partake of it in its fullness. Only when we approach life on all levels do we begin to catch the sparkle, order, beauty, and depth of its many facets.

A police officer once said that it is difficult to compile a reliable record of an accident, because two witnesses rarely give exactly the same report. Furthermore, he said, many witnesses have difficulty giving the same report twice. It is one accident. Certain things do actually happen. But by the time the visual impressions go through the eyes of many witnesses, pass through their minds, become entangled with memories, fright, and deductions about causes and blame, the descriptions are widely varied.

If people respond so differently to something as objective as an accident, how much more likely it is to happen in our responses to the more intangible, philosophical, and subjective factors of life.

Two people watched a beautiful sunset across the quiet evening waters of a large lake, bordered on the distant side by woods. One of them was an artist, and he painted a picture of the sunset. The other said, "The painting is beautiful, but it doesn't look like the sunset I saw." Of course not, for the sunset changed from moment to moment, the colors spreading out, deepening, bouncing off the water and the clouds, drawing together as the sun went farther behind the distant trees, softening, dimming, finally blending into the darkening shades of night. A thousand paintings could not have captured all the blaze of color. As soon as the first visual impressions were recorded in the mind of the artist he began to respond to them. With brushes, paints, and canvas he tried to visualize—for himself, primarily—what the sunset had said to him. He tried to record, perhaps not in any photographic sense at all, what this amazing panorama of beauty and movement evoked in him. But what finally came together on the canvas could not quite match the reflections and emotions of his response to the sunset. His hand, the brushes, and the paints could not be perfect instruments of his thoughts and feelings.

When an observer looks at a painting he usually expects the artist to have painted what the observer saw. He should try to understand that the painting shows what happened to the artist, as the beautiful scene passed into and through him and his response flowed out onto the canvas.

Understanding paintings is difficult but fascinating and enjoyable almost beyond description if we realize that in their works artists respond to any of the myriad aspects of life from viewpoints, angles, and distances that we may never have shared. When an artist looks at a row of apartments with a vacant lot beside them, he does not, like a camera, record fixed lines, surfaces, lights, and shadows as they appear at the moment of exposure. The artist sees that the heap in the vacant lot is garbage thrown from apartment windows, that the garbage cans are overflowing because the sanitation department truck has not come to empty them, that the broken window is a result both of the carelessness of the tenant and the neglect of the owner, and that behind those windows are human misery, wasting childhood, and broken marriage. The silence and the heat, unrecorded by the camera, warn that emotional eruption is about to break out. The policeman at the corner senses it and tries to conceal his inner fear and loneliness in the midst of danger he may not be able to contain. The artist tries to catch these tones and feelings, which are hidden for the most part from the camera and the passer-by. To do this he has to add something, or distort the scene, to reveal his impressions of what the scene says to him. The addition or distortion seems strange to the casual observer, but it may speak deeply to anyone who looks long and sympathetically enough to understand.

Experiencing life on many levels is not limited to painting. The composer takes words, simple or profound, written by another, perhaps centuries ago, and lifts them on wings of tone, rhythm, and harmony never before put together. The music is designed specifically to highlight the meaning of those particular words. We listen. The music passes into and through us, and we respond. We sing! A new dimension is given to life.

Architecture is much more than planning the walls, floors, and roof of a building to keep out the cold of winter and the heat of summer. It is the designing of a fitting environment for engaging persons in a given activity—worship, learning, athletics, banking, or canning sardines. Traditionally, architects have met their greatest challenge in designing houses of worship. Next to churches, perhaps houses of government, colleges, and universities have brought forth the noblest architectural efforts. In more recent years great bridges have been among the most magnificent and spectacular architectural achievements. But anywhere, in museums, office buildings, ships, and automobiles we try to fashion structures that not only serve functions but invite people to engage in them with joy and imagination. While we do it life unfolds.

Why should the church feel responsible for education in the arts? Because Christ came that we might have life and have it abundantly. Life unfolds artistically and always has. Before our response takes the form of paintings, music, poetry, sculpture, or architecture we live in the inner world of imaginings, dreams, wonderment, and awe. What structure of man can begin to match the beauty and magnificence of a night filled with stars? What masterpiece can evoke the human response brought on by the humming of a little child? The first flush of love, the dancing of sunlight on ice-covered branches, the call of a cardinal can set the mind to probing beyond the obvious meanings of life—and the human response moves on the wings of art, or of philosophy, the companion of the arts.

We cannot understand what life is about by approaching it on one level alone. We must see it on many levels, through many eyes, in many dimensions.

Actually, graphic arts may not be the medium through which a given individual will readily find worthy expressions of the experiences of life. He may feel more at home in music, poetry, architecture, drama, or sculpture. Maturity, however, is at least partly the ability to let life speak in many different tongues, and to be able to respond on its own ground.

The church's job is not to deluge children, young people, and adults with more and more pictures, more and more music. Their lives are already saturated with pictures and sounds. The church, in Christian education, should instead expose people to quality and integrity in the arts. This does not mean that biblical art is the only religious art. The artist who interprets the human struggle, defeat, heartache, hope, and need behind the broken window in the apartment house and in the littered vacant lot may be doing something far more deeply religious than the one who paints another head of Christ.

Visits to art museums, to churches that have worthy paintings, windows, and symbols, to places in one's own church where the artistic impulse of the congregation has reached worthy expression, can do much to open a new level of life to people. A little exposure to a few good works of art does more to aid the human spirit in its search for meaning than overexposure to the mediocre.

The church is in the midst of a rebirth of interest in the arts. We have come to understand that an important part of the record of Christianity is in its art, and that an important part of the struggle to understand our time is being contributed by contemporary artists. If, as Christians, we are to make an intelligent and worthy response to the action of God, we must be sensitive to human experience and response on many levels, including the arts.

Children often have a greater capacity to understand art than adults, who have accumulated prejudices and inhibitions. If the adults of a church develop a genuine interest in the best paintings, drama, music, and other arts, they will surround their children and young people with the kind of atmosphere in which a response to many levels of life can grow.

Many churches (often in cooperation with each other) are holding arts festivals as a way of cultivating both art appreciation and artistic expression. A whole new world has been opened to many adults, and certainly to children and young people, through the festivals. There have been festivals of children's art, with remarkable entries of paintings, poetry, and music, and there have been festivals emphasizing more accomplished works of music, drama, and paintings.

Some churches have developed fine collections of reproductions for lending to families. (It is important that these be well mounted and framed, both to protect them and to enhance their message.) Other churches have developed libraries of good reproductions and photographs of other works of art, sculpture and architecture especially, for use in classes to supplement the pictures that come with the curriculum materials.

There are many fine books about art that contain reproductions, many of them in color, that are well worth having in a church library for reference in Christian education.

In Denver, Colorado, a Rocky Mountain Liturgical Arts Association has been formed, and conferences are held to bring together representatives of churches, professional artists, and architects to try to discover areas of cooperative action and concern. This effort has renewed the interest of local artists in the possibilities of working with the churches. Some artists have assisted in the planning of several churches, and others have been commissioned by churches to do some original works of art.

The Board of Christian Education, the church school superintendent, or any concerned individual, can take the first steps in arousing interest in the arts. The matter demands the serious attention of the Christian education leaders.

Some of the new curriculum materials focus attention on art that is worth living with, as well as on high quality illustrative pictures. But not all that is new is good. In fact, the market has been flooded with mediocre filmstrips, motion pictures, and paintings of a "religious" nature. Christian educators need to exercise discernment if children and young people are to be nurtured in the understanding of life—real life—as it is reflected and communicated in the various arts.

Responding to life on only one level reduces a human being to shallowness, reliance on simplified answers to profound questions, and probably a small, self-centered circle of comrades.

Christian education, if it is to be true to the calling of God, who has put us in an infinitely complex, fascinating, and demanding universe, must open for all its students the wonder and joy of attending and responding to him on many levels.

15 *Art Invites Us*

to

Look Again

A mother, her eleven-year-old son, and her
nine-year-old daughter were visiting the south wing of the Chicago
Art Institute. They paused before each painting, commenting
quietly or enjoying it in silence. At one of the paintings the mother
mentioned the name of the artist and said, "Do you remember the
large painting of his we saw in the National Gallery in Washington, D.C.?" They went on and paused at another painting to discuss some of its characteristics. The boy looked up at his mother
and said, "You like it, don't you, Mother?" "Yes," she said. The
visit continued. Obviously this was not their first visit to an art
gallery. The relaxed rapport of this family was beautiful to behold.
As an example of education the children's experience was superb.
They were quietly exposed to the works of accomplished artists and
shared their mother's intelligent interest in good paintings and her
response to them.

At the same time another mother and her daughter of about
twelve were visiting the gallery. The daughter was becoming tired
and restless. Her ability to respond with interest to the paintings
had vanished. The mother said quietly, "You are tired, aren't you?
That's all right, we can go home and come back another day when
we are rested." The mother's sensitivity to the child's fatigue and
her patient assurance that they could come another time opened
the way to other enjoyable experiences with art.

Two young women came into another gallery of the Art Institute, moved quickly from one painting to another, around the room,
and out through the opposite door. One of them tried to linger and
enjoy the paintings, pointing out some of their merits to her friend.

The companion, with a sweeping, cryptic comment about each, disposed of the entire collection within two minutes. This young woman had apparently never been tutored by a parent or teacher with a great appreciation of art.

Another mother and her daughter about seven years old were visiting the museum in the Golden Gate Park in San Francisco. The child wanted to linger at each painting to enjoy it, but the mother kept pulling her daughter along to the next one, saying, "We have a lot more to see." It would have been much better if the mother had lingered with the child, seen half as many paintings on this visit, and returned another day.

Even those people who have the most difficulty responding to paintings probably receive some benefit from their visits, but their experiences suggest the importance of repeated, relaxed, and unhurried viewing of works of art.

What has this to do with the church?

If someone left us a million dollars we would want to be informed of it so that we could acquire the fortune and use it. If someone made arrangements for us to travel around the world, visiting the great art museums and cathedrals, we would want to know about it so that we could leap into the venture. Although a significant part of the world's great art has been brought together in museums for our enjoyment, many churches use these resources in Christian education very little. By taking church school classes and youth groups to the museums, we can travel with them back through history and to many countries of the world at relatively little cost. Probably 65 per cent of the people of the United States live close enough to an art museum to visit it in a day. This percentage is much larger in Europe. On vacation trips, too, many people pass near museums, but hurry on without stopping.

Much of the art in our museums originated through the interest of early churches and individuals. The art has been collected at private expense, and the museums are maintained at no expense to the churches. Not only is this art available at little or no expense, but many museums either have arrangements for guided tours or will arrange them on request. It is best, however, not to take a large group. If a large number must be accommodated on a tour, it is best to divide the group into small units.

One leader sometimes takes her class to a museum to see one

painting in which the students have become particularly interested through their studies. They sit in front of the painting or move about to see it from different positions, discuss it quietly, and ask questions about it. If there happen to be several paintings on the same subject the group may look at all of them. Before coming, the group has learned something about the paintings and artists to stimulate interest, but not enough to lead to preconceived responses.

Visits of this kind can greatly increase interest in the church's collection of reproductions. Interest in art works both ways—having reproductions in the church makes the students want to see the originals, and seeing the originals can help the students look more intelligently at the reproductions.

An appreciation of the world's art can be one of the most important phases of Christian education. The principles emphasized above are also important in visiting churches in order to see their architecture, windows, symbols, sculpture, and paintings, and to listen to great music.

Not all teachers are prepared to lead their students in the experience, and those who are not must have their own interest in art developed. Consequently, developing an openness to art is one of the important aspects of leadership education. Many books on art are available that can be of help to teachers, students, and parents in preparing for visits to art museums and in enjoying the experience.

Many church leaders do not realize what a great resource they have in art museums. In Chicago, for example, the Art Institute can be a part of every church's educational resources. Every church in New York City has many art museums almost at its doorstep, some of them specialized, to serve it educationally. In Washington, D.C., in addition to the National Gallery, there are several other art museums. There are hundreds of art museums and centers in the United States, Canada, South America, Europe, and other areas, in small cities as well as larger ones. In many of them the staffs are willing to assist all the educational agencies of the communities, including the churches.

Children can develop an appreciation of art. Three boys about ten years old were visiting the Metropolitan Museum of Art in New York City. One of them had been there many times and was acquainted with the works of art. While they were having lunch, an adult overheard this boy telling his friends about some of his favorite paintings. Becoming interested in the boy who was so eager for his two friends to see his favorite paintings, she quietly followed them at a distance.

The boy took his friends from gallery to gallery, showing them one or two paintings in each, then leading them on to another. In one place he would explain the subject of the painting and tell his friends about the artist. They listened attentively and caught something of the boy's enthusiasm for the paintings, even if they could not understand all that he said.

The lady followed the boys for some time, and although she was a frequent visitor to the museum, she was able to learn new things about the paintings as she listened to the boy's interpretation of what the works meant to him. She wanted to talk with the boy and learn how he came to know so much about the paintings, but she did not want to break into the delightful experience the boys were sharing. She could imagine that his mother—or it could have been his church school teacher—had spent many delightful hours with him in the museum, sharing her enjoyment of its collections.

If a church school teacher has difficulty enjoying and responding to distinguished paintings, sculpture, architecture, or symbols, he should look again and again, and invite his class to look with him.

16 *The Mark*
We Make

A man walked along the edge of a beautiful city park, stopping frequently to drink from a bottle. Finished with it, he tossed it over the low wall into the park. He was not the first to do it; the park was littered with bottles, cans, boxes, candy wrappers, and newspapers. After walking another two blocks the man suddenly pulled off his topcoat (it was a warm day) and tossed it over the wall, walking on and leaving it there. The man was expressing himself and his attitude toward his community.

A boy wandered through the same park, cautiously concealing an air rifle. Occasionally he raised it and shot a lead pellet at a bird. Fortunately he was a poor shot and the birds escaped. Nevertheless, he was expressing himself and an inner craving for prowess.

Meanwhile, in other places children ice-skated, tossed basketballs, practiced on pianos, read books, wrestled, boxed, and did an infinite variety of things. Whether or not they knew it, they were also expressing themselves and leaving their mark about them. They were exercising their muscles, skills, curiosity, and talents as part of constructive growth, in ways far more satisfying than shooting at birds or littering parks and streets.

Each individual has the right and need to express himself on many levels. Developing skills in many different kinds of activity—athletic, literary, musical, mechanical, scientific, and artistic—allows him to express himself and his ideas more fully. By expressing himself and his ideas he is likely to reach new levels of maturity, and he will be able to communicate with his fellows in ways that bring lasting satisfaction.

Under favorable circumstances a child or young person develops a large range of skills outside the church—at public school, on the playground, in clubs, and in private classes. In the church we must get to know our students and give each of them an opportunity to employ his skills in the development and expression of his Christian experiences and insights. Not all skills have equal appeal to all students, but each person should have the opportunity to express himself even though his skills have not been fully developed.

How does a child learn any skill? How does he learn to use a knife, fork, and spoon? His impulse is to take the food in his hand and ignore the "artificial" tools. He can do an effective, although messy, job of feeding himself that way. Also, when he first tries to use a spoon he is awkward, and, if he could talk, he would probably say, "Oh, I'll never learn to do it!" If, however, he is allowed to handle his food the natural way, with his fingers, he can relate to it quickly.

A young child usually feels awkward the first time he is given a brush, paints, and paper. But if he is introduced to paints and paper and is invited to spread the paint with his fingers and hands, he may be cautious at first, but soon an expression of joy will come over his face as he runs his fingers through the paint, spreading it into various designs. He will be able to relate quickly to the paint as it responds to his will, and he will be able to express his feelings and ideas. As times goes on he may learn to use the tools with equal skill.

If we place a lump of clay and a knife in front of a child, he will probably ignore the tool and start manipulating the clay. In this way the clay quickly becomes an extension of himself so that he understands his relationship to it. He finds that, in an elementary way, he can express himself through the clay. Eventually he may learn to use the tools of the sculptor with more durable material.

If a young person or adult has been unfortunate enough never to have had the opportunity to develop skill as a painter or sculptor, he too can profit by beginning with finger painting and clay molding. If he feels that he ought to be able to use brushes and knives skillfully without first relating to the materials, let him try to eat with chopsticks. He may wish he could lay them aside and dig in with his fingers. Learning to use chopsticks is difficult, even in the simple task of eating. Learning to use paints and brushes, knives and chisels, or the instruments of the musician, as an extension of one's feelings and ideas is, of course, more difficult. But once achieved, the ability to express oneself in any artistic medium significantly enlarges the range of a person's responses to life.

Learning the skills of the arts, even in an elementary fashion, will also increase a person's respect and appreciation for the work of more accomplished artists.

It is best not to push a student too fast in his artistic endeavor. He may not be old enough to undertake it seriously. He may want to play and experiment first with color combinations and forms, or with the beating and molding of clay into fanciful shapes. He may prefer to express himself in writing, drama, poetry, or music. Freedom in selecting the medium and the subject may lead quickly to an ability to relate to them and leave in them the marks of his own feelings and thoughts.

In due time, as his skill develops, he may want to use it to make an artistic comment about life, which, indeed, may end up being religious in nature and value without necessarily dealing with biblical material or the church. It may have to do with life out in the world as he sees it or wonders about it.

A teacher may be able to provide children and young people with paints, crayons, clay, wood, drama, or music, and "turn them loose," but he will be unable to give much guidance unless he himself has had the experience of trying, failing, trying again, and learning to respect artistic endeavor. The teacher need not be an expert, for the artistic effort may be more meaningful to students and teacher alike if they engage in it as companions, rather than as the teacher and the taught.

A group of teachers, who wanted to use arts in Christian education but who had no experience in creative art, got together during the week to experiment. They began with finger painting and molding, then moved gradually toward the use of various art tools. They learned first to release themselves in the endeavor, using whatever skill or medium they found to be the best extension of their own feelings and ideas. As they gained skill they broadened their use of the tools of art. Learning to release themselves and experiment in the companionship of co-workers removed inhibitions and made them feel more comfortable in opening the doors of creative art to their students.

One of the real values of artistic endeavor in Christian education is in opening channels of communication with people of all ages in the church. This is especially true if the people are engaged in artistic expression of some kind, or of several kinds.

Instead of lavishly praising the creative art of children it is better to enter into quiet conversation about it with them. The conversation may turn out to be interesting for the adult, and will be more productive for the child than listening to an adult praising him for work they both know is mediocre. Even if it is mediocre, it may reveal progress, and if these conversations are sincere, they can open to both teacher and student the opportunity to see and feel things about life to which they have not been sensitive before. They can enhance the ability to approach and respond to life at all levels for both young and old.

We have focused our attention on painting and molding, but the principles we have discussed are equally valid in the areas of creative writing, drama, poetry, singing, interpretive movement, choral speaking, or other forms of creative expression. From the simple expressions of early childhood to the more sophisticated statements of adults, Christian education should provide a constantly expanding opportunity for stimulation, clarification of ideas, understanding of feelings and expressing them freely, and learning to approach life and respond to it on many levels.

A local church that has not ventured along these lines of Christian growth has some exciting and surprising experiences ahead. Artistic expression is a natural sort of venture. Primitive people communicated through song, dance, drawing, sculpture, architecture, and painting before a written language existed. Artistic self-expression is one of the privileges that everyone should be allowed to develop in Christian education.

17 *A Highway*
Paved
with Books

There is nothing new about a church having a good library. Some have had libraries for generations, and some denominations have been giving library guidance to their churches for years. On the other hand, many churches have no libraries and seem unaware of how much this lack deprives their members and leaders.

Three major areas of library service are essential to Christian education. It is difficult to put a priority on any one of them, and the order given below has no significance.

Materials for Christian education leaders

Books for the teacher's own development and for his use in teaching should make up a large part of the church library. Some churches place these books in a special "teachers' library" that is easily accessible to the leaders. If there is a minister or director of Christian education the leaders' library should be near his office so that it is readily available to him and his volunteer staff when they are in conference.

New books for this library are coming off the press regularly. At least one person should be given the responsibility for acquiring new books for leaders and for keeping that part of the library up to date.

In most churches, someone should help the leaders and teachers, particularly the new ones, learn how to use the leaders' library and discover how much help can be had from it. Experienced teachers often say that they would not be able to teach effectively without a good resource library.

In one church the picture library is in the same room with the book collection. One Sunday a teacher came to the picture librarian and asked for a picture on a certain subject. The librarian began searching through her index file, but could find no listing on that subject. The teacher felt the nudge of a hand on his arm, but paid no attention because he was trying to help the picture librarian meet his need. Finally he noticed that the book librarian was extending a book toward him, opened to the picture he was looking for. She had overheard the conversation and knew where she could find the picture in her book collection.

When the church adopted new curriculum materials for its church school the book librarian offered to go through all the new materials to see what reference books would be of help in each class. She made up a list of books available for each group.

That librarian was an educational resource in her own right. Not only did she maintain an excellent library, she also provided a helpful consultation service in their use of the library for teachers, students, parents, families, and even the ministers.

The teachers' guidance materials and the adult study courses of the denominational curriculum materials are not designed to be a complete package of all that is needed. They should serve instead as stimulators, interest-whetters, door-openers, and imagination-firers. They are designed to help teachers and students get started and keep moving in their own growth. If the materials are successful, they will arouse curiosity that cannot be satisfied without turning to books, magazines, art, music, audio-visuals, and other resources for further information.

If a church finds that its people are not using the library, it can be sure that its Christian education program does not measure up to the demands of Christian citizenship in the twentieth century. Children and young people need the guidance of adults with rich, growing intellectual interests. They need leaders who are learners, and who teach out of the overflow of their own intellectual activity and spiritual growth. Adults cannot be that kind of leader unless they are reaching for more knowledge and understanding. A church should make the resources for that growth available to them in its library.

Resources for students

A second area of service is providing resource materials for the students in the educational groups. People like to search and find. They remember information they have discovered under their own power longer than information that has been told to them. Many church school teachers have achieved excellent results by guiding students in answering their own questions, rather than handing out easy answers.

Members of one junior high class were engaged in a dozen or more lines of investigation simultaneously. They looked for information about biblical characters. They found out how people dressed in biblical times and whether paintings of them were accurate. They compared versions of the Bible and then turned to books to find out how the different translations were developed. They looked for information about some of the hymns they were using. They read about contemporary issues that were similar to those studied in the Bible. One group in the class studied a few plays based on Bible stories. On and on went the search for interesting and useful information, which they brought together and shared with each other. Their experience in the class was alive and constantly led them forward into new ventures because their leader had ingenuity and imagination in guiding them.

The best curriculum materials open questions and raise issues to which there are no easy answers. Education is more meaningful if the writers do not provide all the answers in the basic materials and if the church is alert enough to provide resource materials.

Students in one church who were guided to such resource materials soon engaged parents and other adults in conversation about their questions, so that there was an opportunity for the adults to make a meaningful contribution to the spiritual venture of the students. After these conversations with the children and young people, the adults often found themselves discussing with each other the live issues of Christian citizenship. Some of their best growth in insight and attitude came as a result of these conversations.

If a church school teacher is making good use of books and magazines in his class, the librarian should allow the class to borrow for a time the materials it needs. Borrowing, however, must not turn them away from the main library. The students should be aware that the church library has more extensive resources beyond the small collection of materials assigned to them. They should not be deprived of the thrill of talking with the librarian about their line of investigation and getting his help in locating the information they need.

Of course, the church library may not have all the resources needed by the members of a class. The teacher or librarian should then suggest that they visit the public or school library. Or perhaps the minister has the information in his personal library. A visit with him about the investigation brings him closer to the students and can pave the way for them to seek his counsel whenever they have personal problems with which he can help.

A unit of study always has possibilities beyond mastering the material given in the basic curriculum guides. These materials raise issues that the students will be facing all their lives. The profound questions of life are not easily disposed of. They are continuously discussed in books, magazine articles, and audio-visual materials. The student will come upon them in motion pictures, plays, radio and television programs, headlines of newspapers, art, lectures, and sermons. The library is not the only source of information about the questions, but it is an important one, to which every person in the church has a right to turn expectantly.

Materials for individual reading

A third important area of service for a church library is providing books and magazines for individual reading. One of the easiest ways to enrich and expand Christian education is to lend supplemental reading materials to members of the education groups.

The primary department of one church developed its own library because the church did not have one and because the leaders wanted their students to have the opportunity to read books of religious value. Parents and friends contributed money for the purchase of books. Many of the children took books home every Sunday and read them during the week. What a difference that made in the information and understanding those children brought with them to church school.

It is important that church leaders discover the interests of their children and young people, encourage them, and help to guide students in those interests. Church school teachers, church librarians, and ministers working together can help to encourage people to develop an interest in reading. A minister's reference in a sermon to a certain book often sends members of his congregation hurrying to libraries and bookstores to get it.

If a church wants to influence the lives of its people, one of the resources at its command is the rich supply of good religious books coming off the presses each year.

Promotion of circulation

It is the responsibility of the librarian, library committee, and church staff to get the books and magazines used once they are in the library. One large city church has an excellent library on an upper floor. There is an item in the budget for support of the library, and many new books are purchased each year. On a table in the reading room is a selection of good magazines. When a new librarian and committee took charge, they discovered that many of the books had never been checked out. Some members of the church had never been in the library, and a few were not aware of its existence. The director of Christian education and the teachers maintained their own small library and made little use of the main library.

The chairman immediately wrote to the leaders asking them to suggest books that would be helpful to their groups, so that the leaders became involved in the selection and promotion of books and developed an awareness of what the library could do for them.

Carefully selected books were then brought down from the library to the social hall to be displayed and checked out during a coffee hour following worship.

The director of Christian education was asked to make her teachers aware of the excellent reference books available. Notices of new books were included in the church's monthly paper and occasionally in the Sunday bulletin. Discussion groups were informed that there were books in the library related to their subjects, and the books were placed on designated shelves.

The remote placement of the library presented a handicap, and the long neglect of promotion had created a disregard for the library that will be overcome only as the new committee and many individuals in the church use imagination and ingenuity to make the library a part of the life of the church.

Each local church has its unique problems in the development of an effective reading program, but each also has its unique resources for the task. Brief book reviews, called teasers, delivered before various groups can call attention to books. Displays of the jackets of new books on the bulletin board help. In many churches there are display cabinets in prominent locations in which interesting arrangements of book jackets can be placed.

Most important in the promotion of reading are the groups and individuals who have discovered that an interesting world of learning exists in the books, magazines, pictures, audio-visual materials, and other resources of the church library. This kind of learning is contagious.

Use of resources
outside the church

Not many churches are able to provide all the resources needed by an active congregation. The librarian and committee should become aware of the resources available from local public libraries, state libraries, college, university, and seminary libraries, and privately endowed libraries. Special needs can be met by turning to them. One person on the committee or library staff can be given the responsibility for learning how books and other materials can be secured from these libraries.

Many denominations and councils of churches maintain audio-visual libraries from which churches may rent films, filmstrips, slides, and recordings. Some public libraries maintain reproductions of fine paintings for lending to churches, schools, and families.

The staffs of many public libraries have demonstrated their desire to serve the churches of their communities. They purchase books of special interest to churches and arrange special shelves of religious books at certain seasons of the year or when the churches are emphasizing a particular subject. They lend collections of books to churches so that the churches can lend them, in turn, to their members.

Sale of books

As an additional service many churches have books for sale. Through this service the people can purchase books that they might not have known about except for the church's bookstore, either for their own reading or for gifts. A few churches maintain bookstores on a year-round basis.

A church may start this service by asking a denominational bookstore for a consignment of books for two or three weeks, perhaps in early December, with the privilege of returning those not sold. The bookstore usually offers a small discount on those sold.

Some churches have developed enough confidence in their ability to select books for which there will be a demand that they purchase the books outright. In this way they receive a larger discount, and, even if a few of the books are not sold, the larger discount more than covers the loss.

One might ask, "Why should a church compete with a commercial bookstore?" It is a good idea, before starting such a venture, to talk with the manager of a local bookstore to discover if he will cooperate in accepting suggestions of books suitable for promotion by the churches. In many local bookstores, unfortunately, the "religious" books are of an inferior quality. If the conversations with the manager are unsuccessful, and if care is taken to select only books of the best quality, the church is then in a position of selling only books that people are not likely to find in the local stores.

A director of Christian education invited a person to come to her church to speak to the church school teachers at their Christmas meeting, soon after Thanksgiving. The speaker suggested that the director arrange with a denominational bookstore for a table of books for sale at the meeting and provided a list of good books. On the evening of the meeting, one of the teachers looked over the books, then asked the director, with some excitement, "Are you going to have this book table here for the women's meeting tomorrow?" The director obviously had not thought of it, but replied, "I think we can hold it over if you want it." "Oh yes," the woman said, "I know that a lot of the women would like to buy some of these books." By the end of the evening the supply was greatly reduced through purchases, but enough were left to make an interesting book selection for the women the next day.

Any church can increase its Christian education substantially through books to use, to lend, and to sell.

PART THREE

Areas for Intensified Learning

18 *Make Sense*
with Senses

Christian educators have traditionally expected their students to learn primarily through the sense of hearing, supplemented in reading with the sense of sight. During the last quarter century there has been a rapid development of projected visual materials, and consequently increased emphasis on the use of sight in learning. Not much emphasis has been placed on the use of the other senses—touch, taste, and smell. But the use of these senses in learning, especially in the enjoyment of learning, is important.

Smell

The senses can make a negative impression as well as a positive one. A boy enrolled in a cooperative vacation church school held in a church other than his own. After the second day he rebelled against going and said to his mother, "The place stinks!" There was a swimming pool in the church near the room in which his class was meeting and the room was not properly ventilated. He was right, the air in the room was unpleasant.

Church rooms that have been closed and unused often have an unpleasant odor if they are not aired out before use. The step from "the room stinks" to "the program stinks" is a short one. A bad odor in a room places the teacher and students under a handicap.

This negative incident is mentioned only to suggest that the sense of smell may play a more important part in learning than we have thought. Not only does a pleasant, fresh smell in a church add to the learner's and worshiper's pleasure in being there; the sense of smell occasionally plays a specific role in learning.

The pleasing and inviting odor of food being prepared for a church family dinner can create a feeling of well-being and add to an appraisal of the church as a good place to be. A pleasing odor of flowers coming through fresh air in a place of worship can enhance the pleasure of being amid beautiful architecture, windows, paintings, and symbols.

The smell of pine branches, burning candles, and flowers in Christmas decorations, and the distinctive fragrance of lilies on Easter Sunday linger vividly in memory. The same scents experienced in other places are likely to bring back recollections of the fellowship and inspiration one experienced at those seasons in his church.

The smell of burning incense associated with the study of ancient ceremonies can help make the learning vivid.

Missionaries often bring home objects that have a strange odor—interesting and pleasant—for use in their visits to churches.

Taste

Closely associated with smell is taste. They are often used together, even when we are not aware of it. Some church school teachers have found that tasting the bitter herbs, honey and apple, fruits and nuts, pastries, spices, and other foods used in ancient Palestine can help students of almost any age understand more intimately the history of early Christianity and its heritage from Judaism.

The enjoyment of foods imported from other countries can easily be associated with the study of the peoples of those countries, their way of life, their industries, their contributions to the arts and literature, and their social problems. Food can be associated with a sense of sharing between those countries and one's own. If these foods have a distinctive odor as well as taste, the two senses together can heighten the feeling of first-hand involvement in what is being learned.

One church had an unusual experience on World-Wide Communion Sunday by having women of the church bring breads made according to the recipes of various countries. Each woman made the bread according to the practice of her ancestral country, learned from her mother or grandmother. The presentation of the breads on the Sunday preceding World-Wide Communion Sunday was carried out in an impressive ceremony, pleasing to the senses of smell, sight, and hearing. On World-Wide Communion Sunday the loaves were broken into small pieces and served in baskets. Each communicant tasted an unusual bread as he partook in the service. This practice was picked up by some other churches with equally interesting results.

Visitors from other countries, or those just returning from other countries, sometimes bring things that have distinctive tastes or odors that are characteristic of those lands. These add a dimension to verbal and visual reports.

Touch

Although touch lacks the delightful sensitivity to the quality of an object provided by taste and smell, it is more impulsively used. "Let me touch it!" is often the immediate response of a child upon seeing something strange or different. Some museum officials, aware of the universal desire to touch and feel things, have arranged certain exhibits so that they can be touched and their texture, coolness, roughness, or hardness can be felt.

The visitor center in the rain forest of the Olympic National Park in the state of Washington contains an exhibit, part of which is behind glass. The exhibit includes the tracks of an animal wandering off into a beautiful setting in the distance. Some of the tracks are placed in front of the glass so that they can be felt. Almost every child and many adults impulsively feel the tracks and rub their fingers into each part of them.

When a missionary to India returned to her home church and wore a sari, the children and many of their mothers wanted to feel the beautiful cloth to become acquainted with its silky texture. She brought many objects with her, all of which the people could handle and feel.

A teacher took her class of children into the sanctuary to study the symbols and architecture. The students ran their fingers over the

carvings to supplement their visual impressions with the understanding that comes through the sense of touch.

Church windows are usually out of reach; but if any portion of
the stained and leaded glass is within reach, touching it will give
an impression of the materials used and the artist's craftmanship
that is almost entirely missed by the visual impression of light
coming through the glass.

Whenever it is possible for a student to touch objects from a
period in history, a country, or a culture, a dimension is added to
the appreciation of what is being explored. Some churches develop
their own collections of objects, symbols, artifacts, sculptures, ancient coins, ancient oil lamps, glassware, dishes, and items of clothing. They keep these in their own museum rooms or exhibit cases
to be taken out for study by various groups. Occasionally some of
them are used in Christmas or Easter ceremonies or on other special
occasions. The children and young people of a church whose leaders are that imaginative and farsighted are fortunate.

Use of all the senses

Christian educators should be alert to the pos-
sibility of using several of the senses in combination in a learning
experience. The object of taste may also have a distinctive fragrance
or odor. It may be significant visually. If the learner can touch and
feel it he may be aware of some of the characteristics of the object
that can be perceived in no other way. He is then able to listen to a
description of the object and the way it is produced and used with
more understanding than would be possible if the information had
come to him only through the sense of hearing. This multiple experience will make him look at the object more carefully and see it
more completely than he could have by using only the senses of
hearing and sight.

Leaders should not overlook, however, in their enthusiasm for
using sight, smell, taste, and touch, the importance of verbal interpretation. One church that had used one pulpit hanging and communion table covering for years because they were memorials,
suddenly began using hangings and coverings of various colors, according to church tradition. The artist in the church who super-

vised it and the minister knew what they were doing, but no explanation was made to the people of the church, and many of them were left puzzled and lacking in appreciation of what was happening.

In contrast to this, a teacher in another church and her class arranged for a unit of study to culminate in a luncheon. They ate foods like those used in ancient Palestine and enacted a Jewish family ceremony. Because all the students participated in the luncheon and in the study that preceded it, they understood what they were doing. Other church school classes have done much the same thing, making the food and the ceremonies as authentic as possible.

In one church a young adult group arranged a series of supper programs through which to become better acquainted with the customs of other peoples. Each supper was prepared or supervised by a guest representing a certain country—Greece, Turkey, Italy, India, Japan, and China. The guest also talked about the country represented, wore clothing of that country, and showed objects of interest. The use of the senses of smell, taste, sight, hearing, and touch in combination made participation in this series of events a memorable experience.

In many churches a single teacher may be imaginative enough to make his own collection of objects to use in teaching. He may arrange for his class to visit museums, churches, and other places of interest where unusual experiences of hearing, seeing, smelling, tasting, and touching may be had. But this is not enough. All the people of a church should have the opportunity to experience with all the senses what they are participating in or learning about.

This is a matter that deserves the attention of the Christian Education Board or Commission, the deacons, the stewards, or other officials of any local church. First, are the rooms of the church aired before they are used so that people will find it pleasant to be in them? Are the rooms attractive visually? Has material been used to prevent unpleasant echoing and reverberation of sounds?

Second, is the church making available to its people, its church school classes, and its young people's groups the things that communicate through the eye (art, audio-visual materials, objects from other lands and periods of history), and through the senses of smell, taste, and touch? Gathering these resources can be a fascinating venture for the people given the assignment, as well as for the learners. Arrangements for the use of resources brought by missionaries and travelers can be made if the church leaders are alert. The appreciative response of the learners is predictable and dependable.

19 *Learning for*

Responsible Living

"People are ready to give money to send missionaries to Africa or India—a 'safe distance away'—but are unwilling to treat members of a minority group in our town as first-class citizens." This kind of statement, heard frequently, points to one of the weaknesses that has characterized Christian education and the church as a whole. It is not that too much emphasis is placed on the world mission of the church. There is too little emphasis and often it is too late. In some churches, however, the interest in "missions," such as it is, has diverted attention from the church's responsibilities next door.

Home-town responsibilities, and questions about the church's own nature and existence, have come crashing in on us in the second half of the twentieth century. It is impossible any longer to ignore them. New nations are coming to independence by the dozens. People who have been discriminated against are rebelling and demanding that they be counted in on the "New Deal," the "Fair Deal," the "New Frontier," the "Great Society," and anything else that is going on.

A minister discovered that a session of his young people's church membership class was meeting at the same time that a prominent speaker was going to address a gathering on civil rights at the public auditorium. Recognizing the importance of the meeting for anyone contemplating church membership, he led his class to the auditorium to hear the address. In the class sessions that followed, discussions took on a dimension and a vitality they would not have had in mere talk *about* the church. The young people found themselves involved as participants in the action of the church on social frontiers. They experienced a responsible kind of learning that put the question of church membership in a new perspective for them.*

Many are proclaiming that the church is irrelevant to the issues of our day. It probably will be irrelevant if it allows itself to be, and if, in complacency, it turns its back on the issues of an emerging civilization.

Emerging civilization? In some future day, the twentieth century may be written off as one of the most uncivilized of all time, however difficult that may be for us to comprehend. It is characterized by savage wars, racial bigotry, illiteracy, starvation, attempted genocide, disease, and indifference to political responsibility. The educational system can hold only a small percentage of its students long enough for them to find out what life is about and to prepare for creative participation in it. The churches' record is even worse than the schools'. There are broken homes, parents who cannot control their children, and disrespect for property and for law. Many people are interested only in cheap entertainment, or in getting from where they are to somewhere else without taking the time to understand who they are or where they are going.

Despite all this, there is a tremendous ferment of possibilities in the world. It is a world of fantastic scientific and industrial development, medical discoveries and skills, new educational and communication media, re-examination of first principles, and struggle for political independence.

In a world of such chaotic conditions and yet such promise it would be inexcusable for the church to take other than a responsible attitude in relation to the issues of the day, or to shirk its work of interpreting life realistically and helping people to live responsibly.

The educational work of the church is not to perpetuate itself as an institution or a tradition, although the institution will probably be perpetuated in the process of doing its work. Christian educators must begin with the student where he is, as he is, recognizing the problems and responsibilities he faces as a part of the human race in this chaotic yet promising world. If Christianity has anything to say to him it must say it to him as a responsible person surrounded by a complex entanglement of issues. Each person is enmeshed in a web of local, regional, national, and world issues from birth. He

---

* *International Journal of Religious Education*, November 1966, p. 14.

becomes acquainted with them gradually as he matures, but he is always a participating member of his community, nation, and world. There is no sanctuary from it. A person may behave irresponsibly as a member of that complex society, but there is no way of escaping the reality of his membership in it.

It is to this person that Christian educators must speak. It is with him that Christian educators must feel, think, and act. The person may be rebellious toward his world, ignorant of his situation, cynical about it, or eagerly searching for understanding and a sense of direction. His particular condition must determine the way the teacher approaches him.

A teacher was trying to present the message of a certain passage of the Bible, when one of the young people muttered, "nuts," and turned to one side as if turning his back on the whole business. In the discussion that followed, almost as an eruption of the individual concerns of the students, the teacher discovered that he had not known his students personally. The discouragement, cynicism, hope, and conviction of various students boiled over for the rest of the session, catching the teacher with a sense of almost complete inadequacy.

The teacher arranged for informal conversations with individual members of the class in order to become acquainted with them. He discovered that the father of one of the students had deserted his family because his wife was having an affair with another man, who had now lost interest. Another boy's father was an officer in the army and wanted his son to have a military career, but the son was inclined toward a position of conscientious objection. This resulted in severe tensions between father and son. One of the girls expected to be married as soon as she finished high school and was wondering if she could wait that long. One boy had been encouraged all his life to take what he wanted by whatever means was necessary. On and on went the variation of situations in which the students found themselves.

The basic message of Christianity and the call to vocation were the same for all the students, but there were wide differences in the way the world looked to them, and in the ways they expected to cope with it.

The problem of being a person of integrity was exposed in the fumbling pilgrimage of each student in such a way that the teacher and student could relate themselves responsibly to each facet of it. A complete solution, of course, could not be found for any of the students, and each had to continue his own search for his role in life. Each, however, could do this with a sense of the concerned comradeship of the other members of the group and the teacher. Each could begin to feel that the Christian message, that had seemed only recently like "the same old stuff," had something to say to him in his unique situation.

Good curriculum materials are a great help to a teacher, but that is not where great teaching starts. It starts instead with the recognition of the student's needs as he tries to discover his responsible role in his family, school, community, nation, and world, and then tries to live with it. God is calling the student to live with him responsibly, to help carry out his unfinished work. The teacher cannot know what that role may be for the individual student, and he must respect the student's integrity in his search for that role, whatever it may be.

Christian educators must deal with the student as he participates in human thought and action, confusion and decision-making, joy and sorrow. What can the church share with him that will give meaning and direction to the student's pilgrimage? What understanding can the church give that will help him deal with the issues of life responsibly?

Good curriculum materials, many supplementary materials, audio-visuals, art, music, and experienced Christians can be helpful to the teacher and those of his students who understand what they are about in the Christian venture and how to use these resources in their undertaking.

We take our bearing from the gospel. It is the reason for Christian education and it is what Christian education is about. The work of the Christian educator, however, begins wherever the student is and finds its fruition only as leader and student become responsible participants in the human venture, with all its problems for them and for mankind as a whole.

20 *Teaching*
in the Midst
of Controversy

The second half of the twentieth century is a time when conflicts and controversies are multiplying and intensifying. To be effective in Christian education we must understand the impact of controversy on people, even those not immediately involved in it. We must know, also, how to take advantage of the educational values controversial issues can provide.

Because many churches have been split over controversial issues, mostly internal ones, some church leaders feel that conflict within a church must be avoided at any cost. "Let's not start a fight!" has been considered wise counsel.

Since the end of World War II hot issues that demand attention have blanketed the earth. Saying "Let's not start a fight" is meaningless. The controversies are here and must be dealt with. Experts in the handling of conflicts have arisen, people who even create them if necessary to gain certain ends. Situations that have smouldered for generations have burst, or been fanned, into flame. Some of the manipulators of conflict are idealistically motivated and others are not. All wait for one conflict to be launched or settled to determine the guidelines for handling the next.

It is an uncomfortable, explosive world in which we live, but it is a world in which issues are sharply, though not always clearly, defined.

Children and young people become involved in many controversies. In some instances they are exploited by one or more parties of a conflict in an effort to gain public sympathy or legal advantage.

Many of the issues that are breaking open deserve the attention of church people. They involve human rights, the development of human resources, the conservation of natural resources, the exploitation of one segment of the population by another, international issues, the responsibilities of governments, controls over distribution of wealth, the development of a responsible citizenry, and many other concerns.

Christian education has entered a new day in which we must perceive the relevance of Christianity to many inescapable questions. Christian educators must help children, young people, and adults recognize the existence of conflict and controversy, and the inevitability of tension if society is to move forward. They must help their students learn how to participate constructively in controversies, and to handle their feelings so that individual growth can take place.

This places a great responsibility on Christian educators, for they must learn to handle their own feelings objectively in order to help their students gather the information that can bring enlightenment. The illumination of an issue with dependable data, objectively gathered and viewed, can eliminate unmanageable anger that only frustrates attempts at understanding.

Two groups, well balanced in the quality of their membership and leadership, were asked to discuss a certain issue. A minimum of information was given to one, but the other was given abundant data about the issue. Group one soon ran into a log jam of intense and unmanageable feelings. Factions developed and solidified. The factions found it difficult to talk with one another, and the group broke informally into several subunits, each trying to buttress its arguments.

Group two also developed intense feelings but turned to the data that had been made available. Some individuals began to change their opinions and their feelings about them in the light of the information. This group broke, more formally, into subunits, each charged with the responsibility for studying a body of information carefully and reporting back to the larger group. The subunits were allowed to choose their assignments, and these choices criss-crossed the lines of feelings expressed earlier in the discussion. The group was well on its way toward arriving either at a solution that all could accept or at an acceptable statement of alternative possibilities for solution. In the process, all could grow in understanding and in the management of feelings.

One of the objectives of Christian education should be to help each student learn how to deal with conflicts without becoming submerged in the controversy—in other words, how to be the third party in a tense situation. Role playing * can help young people and adults learn how to be the third party in a conflict situation. Learning how to be the third party also helps an individual learn how to manage his own feelings, and therefore his constructive contribution, when he takes a stand on an issue.

In relation to public issues, a church has the responsibility for contributing to an unemotional and objective, but still forthright, approach to a problem, and it must consider all the related documentation essential to a solution.

One church school class developed into something of a laboratory training ground for dealing with controversial issues. Some issues intruded into the group conversation and were dealt with rather than avoided. Others were introduced that needed further study and deliberation. Early in the experience the leader helped the group understand the futility of trying to work through a controversial issue without relevant data. Sometimes role playing was used to objectify feelings about an issue and help the group look at it on its merits.

For a while there was a tendency to brand individuals as conservative or liberal, to identify them consistently with a particular view of things. Research assignments brought factual illumination into emotionally charged situations and helped prevent the group from characterizing its members in rigid roles. Individuals with strong opinions were sometimes asked to gather data supporting positions opposite to their own.

As a result of this experience, the members of the group learned to look at all sides of an issue while making up their minds about it, so that when the time came to take a stand, it was done constructively, with the merits of the issue objectively considered.

The earlier in the consideration of an issue the information about it can be introduced the better. It is easy for parties in a conflict to become so locked in by their feelings that they are incapable of accepting objective data. Behavior can become so irrational that the only solution seems to be for one side to mount greater power than

* See *How To Use Role Playing Effectively,* by Alan F. Klein (New York: Association Press, 1960).

can be mustered by the other. Considering relevant information early, before feelings have become intense, tends to keep the heat low and the doors open to objective contemplation and negotiation.

Great public issues, such as fair and equitable treatment of ethnic and racial minority groups, sometimes sweep everyone into controversy in one way or another. When this happens, the larger the number of people and groups who have turned to the objective study of the issue, of the data related to it, and of possible solutions, the better. This makes it important for all church groups to be constantly engaged in the study of controversial issues. A group that has made a careful study of the facts about discrimination in housing, employment, political representation, and education, for example, is in a position to become part of the solution instead of contributing to the intensification of the problem.

In the process of informing themselves for responsible participation in the solution of an issue, the members of a group often find that their study is intensely educational. If they have considered biblical and theological insights as relevant data, they can experience a down-to-earth Christian education that is meaningful and practical. They can also gain a new understanding of the relevance of the Christian gospel to the issues of contemporary life.

If church groups all across a nation would approach controversial issues in this objective way, their influence on the actions of government and of the parties in a controversy could be noteworthy.

Any church that wants its Christian education ministry to count in the lives of its people must recognize the educational potential of controversial issues. Instead of avoiding conflicts, it can equip its people, old and young, to be influential participants and third parties in controversies by bringing together the information essential to an understanding of the issues. Sometimes this also means bringing resource leaders into the discussion to interpret the data.

References to issues and information about them in sermons, forums about the issues, references to books available in the church library, research assignments in church and church school groups, papers prepared by persons participating in the study, and even drama can stimulate an objective approach to an issue.

Sometimes a policy question within a church becomes controversial. Such a conflict is not to be avoided at all costs. Rather, the situation can become a laboratory in which the members of the church can test the principles of Christian love and understanding in the process of seeking the right solution. Even when objective information relative to the issue is studied, genuine conflicts of interest may arise. It is often impossible to escape the reality of intense feelings about a problem. It is better to recognize these feelings and accept them than try to "hush them up." If the members of the church can maintain their determination to work through the problem with complete openness of discussion and democracy of action, it may come through the conflict stronger than before.

In one church two issues became intensely controversial, the second arising soon after the first had been settled. In each instance feelings became so intense that the minority faction tried to mobilize pressure and voting power greater than that of the majority. But the church was able to maintain such openness and frankness that afterward most people felt that the issues had been settled with fairness to all concerned. The breaches quickly healed, with little loss of membership. The church was probably stronger after the controversies than before.

Controversies can arise within a single church group. In one group, the two persons around whom the conflict polarized, and who were on a head-on-collision course, managed to talk out the problem so thoroughly that they felt closer to each other than to any other members of the group. This fact helped other members to work their way through the problem to a solution.

A church that is alive with reference to controversial issues and is carefully studying the information available about them is likely to be an educationally alert, excited, and effective church.

No church can afford to overlook the educational possibilities presented by controversial issues, nor its responsibility in relation to them. The multiplication of such issues in our time is disruptive to social order, but intensifies the climate of expectancy, expands the growing edges of social change, and increases the areas of Christian education.

21 *Space Limitations*
Can't Stop Us

Whenever a new venture in Christian education is suggested some person is likely to protest, "We don't have the space and equipment for it!" Churches may think they do not have enough space when actually they do have it, and then use the supposed lack of space as an excuse for not improving their Christian education.

In examining the use of its building and equipment a church should keep certain basic principles in mind to make sure that the best use is being made of whatever space and equipment is available. If, after full use is being made of the building there is still inadequate room for a needed program, a church can turn to ways of supplementing its accommodations for meetings.

Full use of all space

Churches tend to fall into traditional patterns of organization and room use. Regardless of the size of the church school it is likely to be organized into the traditional departments: nursery, kindergarten, primary, junior, junior high, young people, and adult, or some combination of these. As a result, some rooms may be used to half their capacity or less and others may be crowded.

In one church a women's class that had become old with the years and small with the death of many of its members was firmly established in the church parlor, while the young people were crowded into a small room. Finally the women were persuaded to relinquish the parlor to the young people if the church would furnish a smaller room with comfortable chairs.

The same church discovered that a basement room that had never been finished and was used only by a Boy Scout troop could be made into a fine clubroom and still be used by the Scouts. The Scouts were provided with adjacent storage space so that their equipment need not be kept in the clubroom. The church also found that by reassigning various departments of the church school to different rooms, and removing two small partitions in one room, every department could have better accommodations than it had been using.

Another church, with a building about forty years old, had never finished a large space in the basement. The room was finally finished and made into a beautiful assembly hall and dining room that was the most attractive room in the building. Forty years late!

Many churches have discovered that a room that had been cluttered with odds and ends of old furnishings could be made into an attractive classroom or clubroom.

Multiple use of the building

Because a church building is usually used most fully on Sunday morning, we tend to think primarily of its use by the church school, choirs, and other groups meeting at that time. We need to think of the weekday uses of a building just as forthrightly as we think of the church school. Preparing the building for the use of weekday groups brings to the forefront many problems that are just as real, though perhaps not as noticeable, on Sunday morning.

Church committees and architects planning a new building or the remodeling of an old one often speak of a "multiple-use room," a "multiple-purpose room," or an "all-purpose room." Usually they refer to a dining room or assembly hall. Actually, nearly every room in a church should be a multiple-purpose room. We need to plan for a multiple-use building, not just a single all-purpose room within the building.

A medium to medium-large room, providing 25 to 35 square feet per person and large enough for 20 to 25 people, is used more easily for various activities than a small room. Such a room provides space for a church school class to move around in, and is large enough for a Boy Scout, Girl Scout, or Camp Fire group, a board meeting, a young adult group, small suppers and luncheons, and many other activities throughout the week.

Rooms arranged in suites are often the most useful. Next to or near a large or medium-size room it is a good idea to have one or more smaller rooms where committees or subunits of a club can meet. Too often all the smaller classrooms are grouped together, one after another along a hall, instead of being distributed.

One church, in remodeling, arranged on one floor a room 28' × 40', with two rooms 13' × 18' across a hallway. There was a double door into each of the smaller rooms, and two double doors into the large room, making it possible to open the three rooms into one large suite. Privacy could still be preserved when each room was used separately. On the same floor was another room 18' × 25', two washrooms, a kitchenette, coatrooms, and several storage spaces, making the floor into an excellent multiple-purpose area for use throughout the week.

On another floor in the same building is a recreation room 35' ×50', two rooms 17' × 20', three smaller classrooms, a kitchenette, two storerooms, and some storage closets and chests. Two departments of the church school use the rooms on Sunday morning. A young people's fellowship uses the two medium-size rooms and the kitchenette on Sunday evenings, while two adult groups alternate in the use of the recreation space. Scout groups use the suite of rooms and some of the storage space during the week.

Conveniently arranged storage for each group using a room adds greatly to its usability. There should be storage space nearby for adult chairs and tables while a room is being used by young children, and for children's furniture while adults are using it. Some churches have discovered the convenient arrangement of having a chair and table storage cabinet 36 to 40 inches high in one wall, with shelf cabinets above it divided for use by different groups. Some people prefer stacking chairs to folding chairs, but these call for walk-in storage space rather than the cabinet arrangement. The chairs are stacked on a dolly and rolled into the storage room.

Small storerooms, closets, and cabinets, distributed at convenient locations in a building so that equipment need not be moved far, are preferable to a large central storage area.

Adjustments in both rooms and program organization can often be made so as to secure the maximum use of a building. Sometimes it is best to try to find ways to adapt the building to the program, even to the point of thoroughly remodeling the building. On the other hand, especially in the Sunday church school, departments and classes can sometimes be organized in sizes to fit the available rooms, so as to make maximum use of the space available. There is nothing sacred about a particular division of a church school into departments and classes. Although a certain arrangement may be advantageous if there is no problem in accommodating the groups, this arrangement can be changed if it means that the rooms can be used more efficiently.

The major concern is that each group have plenty of space for a varied program of fellowship, worship, study, and activity. If possible, the younger groups should have 25 to 35 square feet per pupil and teacher, whereas a minimum of 20 to 30 square feet per person should be provided for junior high and older. For working groups during the week and Scout and other club activities, 25 to 35 square feet per person is essential, plus storage space. If there is not this much space for the usual enrollment of a group it is best to have more units with a smaller membership in each, even if it means having them meet at different times.

The attractiveness of rooms is a most important factor. For the program to be effective there should be good room atmosphere. Light colors on the walls make them attractive and make the room seem larger. Splashes of bright colors, tastefully arranged, can add warmth and cheeriness to a room. Even a small church can make its rooms attractive if leaders and parents are concerned.

If a group is reading, writing, sewing, or doing other close work, adequate overhead lighting is essential. In the daytime there should be more artificial light on the side of the room away from the windows than on the side near the windows, in order to have equal light in all areas. Table and floor lamps add warmth and a relaxed, homelike atmosphere to a room. Often an attractive, clean rug on the floor reduces noise and makes a room more attractive and inviting. Good reproductions of two, three, or more paintings open up a room, giving it a dimension it would not have otherwise, and adding point to the atmosphere. A piano, record player, television set, book table, and other furnishings can be added if they are appropriate and if there is room for them.

Longer church school sessions

Habit can be a deadening thing. Perhaps none has been more devastating than the habit of holding the Sunday morning church school for only one hour. In many churches the possibility of a longer session never seems to have entered the heads of the leaders. Yet other churches have been holding two- or three-hour church schools for years. One of the ways to make full use of a church building is to hold a longer session of the church school. Even a one-and-a-half-hour session can add immeasurably to the effectiveness of the school, as compared with a one-hour session. Anyone who has worked in a vacation church school, day camp, resident camp, or Scout group can testify to the value of the added hours and the education they make possible.

Christian education is spreading out

With new features being added to the Christian education program, even churches with large buildings may find that they have inadequate space. Regardless of the size of a church, its building may not have been planned for the kind of Christian education program needed today.

Some churches now hold the church school, or part of it, during the week instead of on Sunday. Others hold two complete schools, one on Sunday and the other during the week. By having fewer students on Sunday, they have more space per person and are able to do many things that could not be done under crowded conditions. In some churches the weekday school meets on one afternoon or on Saturday. In others, part of the classes meet in the afternoon after school, followed by a church family dinner, then a family service of worship. Many of the churches holding weekday church schools and worship services report larger enrollment and better attendance during the week than on Sunday. All such branching out of Christian education also works toward a fuller use of the building.

Churches that are extremely limited in facilities have had success in having some classes, or all of them, meet in homes in the neighborhood. Normally, it is easier to have young people and adults meet in homes than young children, for whom small chairs and tables or other special equipment needs to be provided. Meetings of committees and Christian education leaders can be held in homes. Cub Scouts normally meet in homes.

Most churches make very little use of the churchyard for anything except parking cars, but the churchyard, with a bit of imagination and planning, can be made a great asset. Picnics, outdoor recreation, vesper services, outdoor receptions, classes, and many other gatherings are held by some churches on the lawn.

The Congregational Church of the Chimes, in Van Nuys, California, grew very rapidly and had to hold much of its church school on the lawn until its building program could catch up with the growth of membership. It reports that the venture brought satisfactory results and made it possible to provide classes for all who came. An adult class met on a patio under a huge tree for coffee and a study and discussion program each Sunday. True, this was in California, but other churches in mild climates have done the same thing, and many churches in the North could take their classes out of hot, stuffy rooms during the summer, to the shade of the building or of trees, and have an inspiring setting for fellowship and study.

Special summer activities

However inadequate its building may be, or seem to be, a church with limited space is under no handicap when it comes to special summer activities such as day camp, vacation church school, resident camps and conferences, leadership education schools and conferences, and visits to museums and other centers of interest. Some of the best Christian education takes place in these activities.

The importance of the building

The above comments are not intended to suggest that all Christian education takes place in the church building. The emphasis in preceding chapters, again and again, has been on the role of Christian education in the whole life of the student, throughout the week, in his relations and responsibilities in the home, school, playground, at work, in the community, and in the whole world. God is at work in all the affairs of men, and what happens in a church building is significant only in relation to Christian learning and action in the whole of life.

These comments are made because the Christian education that is carried on in the building can be made more or less effective by its setting. The church building is one of the places where learning takes place. The simple fact that it is a church building does not guarantee that the learning that takes place there will be the kind that will help the student grow and mature as a Christian. A building that induces disrespect for the program and leadership rather than participation and responsible human relations can have a negative influence. A building planned as suggested above can encourage the kind of involvement and learning that carries over into the whole of life.

The Christian Education Board, Commission, or Committee ought to maintain a continuous evaluation of the building and its effect on Christian education. In one church the Christian Education Committee had been conducting such an evaluation. When a member of the Board of Trustees raised a question about possible modernization the chairman of the Christian Education Committee had facts at hand and was able to make a convincing presentation of them that led to extensive modernization. This could not have been done without preparation.

Leaders who are alert to the importance of the building's effect on Christian education will see many ways in which rooms and facilities can be improved and better used as a setting for Christian education. A church that is caught up—the whole family of the church—in Christian education is likely to make its building a useful base from which to operate.

22 Then There Is the Whole Out-of-Doors

A male cardinal on a high branch called to his mate. Three bluejays scolded in another tree. Robins sang a rich chorus from near and far. People sitting on benches along the edge of the park paid no attention to the birds. They had not trained their ears to catch their songs. Two boys went by, one of them carrying a turtle. A woman wrinkled her face at it and let out a sound resembling "ugh!" The other boy talked passionately about oceanography and the ocean's tremendous resources of food, minerals, and water that will have to be used as the population expands.

The boys would go to a church camp in July. An older couple sitting on a bench would be invited soon to attend a church camp for older adults to be held during the summer.

For many years churches have conducted camps and other outdoor programs, but in recent years a new philosophy of Christian education in the out-of-doors has been developing. The range of the outdoor program is expanding rapidly. There are outdoor activities for children, young people, students, young adults, families, adults, and older adults. There are resident camps, wilderness camps, trail camping, day camping, canoe trips, wilderness hikes, weekend retreats, and exploratory ventures on farms, in parks, and in churchyards.

Why is all of this important? Why is Christian education in the out-of-doors receiving such emphasis?

The beginnings of it

For many centuries men have lifted up their eyes to the hills, the sunsets, the rushing waters and felt closer to the great power and spirit back of creation. As church camping developed the most remembered "hilltop" experiences were in the vesper services, held as the sun settled beyond a lake or a forest, painting the sky with an ever-changing glow of colors. Inspiration was central in the camp experience.

Then came a new kind of camp leader who saw in the out-of-doors many important things besides sunsets. Through the years campers had gone to outdoor conference centers largely unaware of the great variety, depth, beauty, and orderliness of the natural life all about them. They attended classes, went swimming and boating, put on talent shows, ate, ate, ate, sang around the campfire, held ceremonies, and worshiped out of doors if sitting on the ground was not too uncomfortable. The new camp leaders, however, have labored long and faithfully to turn the mind of the church toward the more profound experience of discovering how God operates creatively and redemptively in the natural world, and the essential relation of human existence to that world.

Men have exploited nature, slashing through her forests and laying them waste, ripping up her soil and letting it erode away, exterminating much of her wildlife on which humanity ultimately depends, and devouring her mineral resources in the mouths of industry, construction, commerce, and transportation. Slowly men are realizing that there is a vital, life-and-death relationship between man and the natural world. We are dependent on that world, and our waste, destruction, and pollution of it have become more threatening as the great increase in population has gotten under way. Men are beginning to discover that God considers the natural world more important than they had thought it to be. There is a marked increase in responsible action on the part of many industries as well as conservationists.

With urbanization, industry, and highways absorbing more and more land area the need for understanding nature, for cultivation, development, and conservation of natural resources, for restoring a balance between humans and wildlife, and for proper use of nature's gifts has become imperative. Man must discover himself, not as the looting king of the natural world, but as a being whose very existence depends on his respect for that world and his reverence for the creative force at work in and through it. The church can play an important part in helping men to mature in their relation to all of creation.

The education of curiosity

Curiosity can kill the cat, break windows, lead to drug addiction, bring about unhappy marriages, and open the door to all sorts of frustrations. On the other hand, it can be one of the most powerful factors in human development. Life in the out-of-doors, if planned for the education of curiosity, can be the setting for a most enjoyable and productive learning experience. It can open to young and old a view of creative and redemptive action even more inspiring and beautiful than the sunset. We can see that action, hold it in our hands, look at it through a magnifying glass, care for it, and cultivate it.

The wilderness camp, the trail camp or hike, the exploration of the out-of-doors in day camps and wilderness hikes are particularly suited to the satisfying of disciplined curiosity. However, increasing opportunities for understanding our natural environment are being provided in many resident camps and conference grounds.

The stimulation and guidance of curiosity about the nonhuman world and its manifestations of universal principles is needed through the year, in all seasons, but can be enlarged and enjoyed especially when church groups go into the out-of-doors.

The human relations involved

However full and wholesome relations in a home may be, the members of a family should venture out of doors (1) to discover new dimensions of their own family life, and (2) to experience associations with people of the larger human family under conditions permitting the formation of deep acquaintances and understanding. Several days spent out of doors in a family camp or an age-group camp offer unequaled opportunity for the development of personal friendships.

There are several factors that make an outdoor venture the setting for effective learning:

1. Spending five to ten days, or even a weekend, in informal fellowship, discussion, recreation, study, worship, and eating together causes people to discard the masks they normally wear, and expose themselves to each other as they rarely do back home.

2. The nearer a group comes to the natural world in these experiences the more easily the masks are shed and the more deeply people come to know each other. A group does not have to import all of its program to the camp. Much of the substance of its study, work, fellowship, and recreation is already there to help the campers discover how deeply the processes of creation and redemption are involved and clearly revealed in the natural world.

3. The experiences of communal living, of interdependence, of respect for other people, of sharing responsibilities can be had in the out-of-doors to a profound degree if leaders and campers understand how to form and conduct a camp community. The groups should be relatively small. If it is necessary to accommodate a large number the camp should be organized into unit communities of twenty to thirty. The unit should be small enough so that each individual can come to know every other with some depth of understanding. The units can enter into certain events together to provide a sense of fellowship in the larger community.

The year-round experience

Most church camps have been conducted by area organizations, denominational and interdenominational. These have their place; they make certain contributions that no local church can make itself, especially in leadership and in associations with people from other countries. But there are also advantages in having the campers know each other in a year-round program in a local church before coming to camp. This is one of the reasons for the local Scout unit going to camp as a group. The week or more at camp is part of the group's year-round program.

The educational and recreational program carried on by the New York City Mission Society, for example, includes programs at four summer camps, but it also includes an extensive program of education, recreation, crafts, music, and fellowship throughout the year. Consequently, children and young people already know each other as they go to camp, and many of them have developed meaningful friendships.

Churches should consider the many possibilities of providing this kind of year-round program. Some churches can afford to own their own camps, but this is not essential. Hikes, day camps, trail camps, canoe trips, the exploration of parks, forests, churchyard, and other natural sites nearby can provide a great enrichment of the areas of common experience, personal understanding, and enlightenment about the natural world.

The ground-level view of God's creation

Great emphasis has been placed on the wilderness as a place to get away from the hustle and bustle of the world. Church groups have "retreated" to camps to be "away from things," to take a fresh look at themselves. Unfortunately much of the time has been spent looking at the things from which they fled. What can we get away *to* in the out-of-doors?

Recreational use of forests, mountains, streams, lakes, and seashores that does not damage natural resources is legitimate and to be encouraged, quite apart from the kind of discovery described above. Outdoor settings are inviting for conferences even when minimal attention is given to the natural surroundings. Many of the values of fellowship and concentrated study are enhanced by the setting. Nevertheless, the most important thing about getting into the wilderness is the opportunity to come face to face, hand to hand, mind to mind with God at work in his natural world, and to come to understand what his creative and redemptive action says about us.

The creation story in the Bible is concise and interesting. The story of creation can be learned with equal interest in the tremendous drama of life in streams, lakes, and ocean, in the formation of land masses and soil, in the restoration of a forest after a fire, in the preservation of balance in wildlife when man leaves it alone, in the evidences of early sea life far inland, in the effect of glaciers in the formation of a continent, to mention but a few of the many manifestations of the creative and healing process.

If it were not for the re-creative and healing power built into the physical world man's abuses quite likely would have destroyed his environment long ago. This is a sobering thought.

Coming close to God's everlasting creative and re-creative action in the out-of-doors has helped people young and old to learn important things about themselves, about human relations, about responsible decision-making, about helping anyone in need. It has also helped them to develop a new kind of respect for life and a reverence for him who is the author of it.

23 *Let's Make It Ours, Too*

When a person accepts an assignment to lead a Christian education group of any kind—church school class, youth fellowship, Scout group, or an adult or young adult study group— the major factor in the situation is the exposure of the leader and the group to each other. What the leader *is* is far more important than what is in the resource books. What flows out of his life in his relations with the students is what counts. The teacher had better be sure that it is authentic Christianity. If he is not sure of it he should be frank in admitting it and in searching with his students for a Christian perspective and commitment.

Many would say that the first qualification of a teacher is that he has Christian conviction and commitment—that he *is* a Christian. They would say that a second qualification must be a concern for the students and an understanding of them. A third qualification, however, may be more important than either of these. It is an eagerness on the part of the leader to learn, to inquire, to listen, to discover. This youngness of spirit, desire to press beyond the known, is captivating and contagious. Students respond to it. Given a leader with this eagerness to learn, he and the students will develop a concern for one another. They will develop a deep understanding of each other. Out of their searching they stand a good chance of arriving at a Christian point of view, conviction, and commitment.

One leader found himself engaged in this kind of exploration and search with a class. Soon he was driven by the demands of the group to study the resource books thoroughly in order to have a reflective grasp of the subject matter. Before long he discovered that doing this alone was not enough, and he sought the fellowship of other teachers, in which he might probe with them more deeply into the subjects being studied. Together they sought the help of the church librarian, who was able to suggest interesting and helpful additional resources, some from the church library and others from the public library. These were read and shared.

The teachers together discovered that the issues the students were facing and exposing in class discussions were the same issues adults faced. The teachers and students met the issues on different social levels, and they dealt with them from different levels of experience, but the insights of the children and young people were often as profound as those of their teachers—and more frankly stated.

The gospel became something the teachers and students could discuss honestly and frankly. Doubts and disbelief could be shared. Understanding could be developed tentatively, then with conviction, rather than as a pious pretense.

Participation in the whole life of the church came to mean more to the teachers because they found that other members of the church were bothered by the same problems that engaged the attention of the teachers and their students. Some of the teachers drew other members of the church into the class discussions. This provided a profitable experience, both for the visitors and the members of the classes. It gave the students a new appreciation of the church's adult members. They were "all right" people, after all, not insincere pretenders. As a result of this the children and young people began to participate more regularly in congregational worship and other church functions. They began to have the feeling that "this is our church, and its work is our responsibility."

When it was suggested that the teachers attend a community-wide leadership education school, some of them decided to go. Maybe they would learn something about the gospel and how to dig deeper into it with the students. They did. A seminary Bible professor taught a class during the first period of the evening, and during the twelve sessions a new perspective was opened to them on the meaning of some of the most puzzling portions of the Bible. They began to understand the Bible as they never had before.

During the second period each evening they took courses in methods of teaching. They received a brief but helpful introduction to the use of extra reading, field trips, drama, role playing, audio-visuals, puppetry, creative writing, creative art, the appreciation of art, and many other ways of living with a subject to broaden and deepen their understanding of it.

Not all of the teachers attended the school. Those who did were so enthusiastic that they suggested to the church school superintendent that what they had learned, and more they wanted to learn, be brought to all the teachers through seminars and a workshop in their local church. These were arranged, and a larger number of the teachers attended. The teachers were permitted to bring their own children to the workshop sessions, and they soon found that the children could teach the adults many things about certain learning procedures—things they had learned in public school.

Out of this experience grew an arrangement for a teacher from another church, with outstanding experience and insight, to visit some of the classes and make suggestions to the leaders and students on how to improve their work. This was enlightening, and the students appreciated being treated on the same level as their adult leaders. Their enthusiasm for their studies was increased, because they saw a new dimension to their significance. Furthermore, they were impressed by the seriousness with which their leaders took their responsibility.

The next summer the denomination held a large Christian education conference on a university campus several hundred miles away. Announcement of it was made, and the church offered to pay expenses for any teachers who could go. The teachers looked at one another, and some said they would think about it. Three carloads went, including a few nonteaching husbands and wives. Lectures, demonstrations, exhibits, seminars, and informal conversations carried all of them to a new appreciation of the importance of Christian education, not only for the individual student but for the nation and the world.

The people went home tired, yet refreshed in outlook. Their suitcases were bulging with new books.

What had happened to these Christian education leaders? From their initial experiences of studying resource materials, to conversations with other teachers and with others in the church, to the training school, the workshops and seminars, and the national conference, the leaders had been finding out that the gospel of Christ which they had been commissioned to teach they first had to experience themselves.

At first it was an exciting venture, full of surprises and discoveries. It was not long before excitement seemed not quite the word for it. True, it was exciting, often thrilling, but the experience was more profound than those words suggest. The experience of the gospel led them into a new understanding of what life is probably about —what God, in his creative imagination, may be driving at. They were never quite sure that they understood, but at least they felt that they were on the edge of a magnificent mystery—and faith!

"This is no longer something they tell about in the resource books," said one of the teachers. "It has to be ours, too, if we are going to share it with our students."

Any church that seriously wants to provide solid Christian education for its people, old and young, must provide opportunities for its Christian education leaders to develop their own Christian faith and understanding. Growth ought not to be expected of children and young people that is not expected of their parents and teachers. Growth ought not to be expected of the parents and teachers that is not expected of the church officials and members. All need to say, "Let's make it ours, too!"

24 Curriculum

from

the Inside Out

We cannot buy and import a curriculum. We can acquire curriculum resources—printed materials, audio-visuals, art, drama, music, even guest leaders—but these are not the curriculum of Christian education.

The starting point of Christian education is in the life of a congregation itself, as the people give heed to the gospel of Christ and respond to it. As a congregation seeks resources for Christian education it must look first for resources for its own enlightenment, spiritual nourishment, and strengthening in its work in the world.

The people a church would teach are part of itself and its own life. If a church attempts to teach its children and young people without trying first to learn and grow, it is setting the students apart as something other than itself. It is saying, "I have it and you do not, so I shall teach it to you." This is a false position. All of us are "standing in the need of prayer," information, interpretation, inspiration, re-education, retraining, discipline, repentance, and forgiveness. The love of God, as revealed in Christ, is so tremendous that even the wisest among us can touch only the hem of it. All of us, old and young, must be bound together in a worshiping, learning fellowship.

For good or ill a congregation provides the curriculum of Christian education. What happens to the children, young people, and adults within the church is the curriculum. Everything that a church does, in the institution and out in the world, is part of its teaching action. Many of the actions of a church influence students more than what happens in the classroom. What individual church members do in their relations with each other, in their associations with children and young people, and in their work and social life may say more to the students than what is taught in the classroom. The ball batted over the fence into a garden or through a window may give an adult the opportunity to show the players more about human understanding, patience, and affection than a hundred church school lessons.

Curriculum materials are not the primary thing in Christian education. They are tools, means to an end, not an end in themselves. We need as curriculum resources (and worship resources) the kind that will help all of us learn, grow, and serve.

When we look for materials, we should ask ourselves "What is our need? What resources will help us most?"

In asking these questions we recognize that the materials needed by people of different ages and experience vary. Materials should be designed for the special needs and interests of the various age groups.

The fact is, however, that many adults are still facing elementary questions and never have found the answers to them. Let us not be deceived by age—even our own! Essentially, most of us are still facing the basic questions that children face: Who am I? Where did I come from? Why am I here? Where am I going? How do I operate in this complex world? For what am I responsible? We are searching for the materials that will help us, old and young, find answers we can live by.

In evaluating its Christian education program a church must look beyond its curriculum resources, important as they are, and examine its whole life. If there is weakness at its heart, it cannot make up for that by erecting a Christian education building and importing a curriculum. It must ask, rather, "Do we believe the gospel we preach and teach? Do we make this apparent in the attitude we show to people, old and young, of all races and nations?"

In our efforts to be the kind of fellowship that radiates our response to the message of Christ, we turn to materials and other resources to assist us in our growth, knowing that we, first of all, need Christian education. It is only as we ourselves have the experience of redemptive love that we can share this kind of life with persons coming to us for Christian education. We need materials that will help us grow in our own hearing of the gospel and response to it, as well as in our ability to interpret it to others.

Denominations are making a great effort to provide the kind of curriculum and leadership materials that will be most helpful. They have made great progress in recent years. They have secured the help of Bible scholars, theologians, educational psychologists, artists, sociologists, and researchers.

While some local churches are making only half-hearted use of the new materials, others have used them and found a new understanding of what it means to be a church.

One church, in adopting the new materials its denomination had prepared, discovered that the Christian education proposed in these materials must start with adult leaders and parents. Some of the teachers dropped out rather than undertake the program of study into which they were invited. To replace them, parents who were challenged by the new concept of Christian education volunteered. The teachers and the parents who became involved began to see Christianity as well as Christian education in a new light. As they came to understand more clearly the meaning of the gospel they examined their response to it in their own lives. They saw that simply meeting children and young people in the classrooms was not enough, and they went to the other parents with their concern for the whole pilgrimage in which old and young alike were engaged. Many parents began to respond. Some who had taken the church lightly began to see that there was a responsibility they could not treat as optional. The life of that church is deepening and growing as the children, young people, and adults sense their oneness in the Christian life and mission.

When a church tries to develop a vital approach to its own being and mission, it becomes aware that it needs many resources beyond the denominational curriculum materials. These latter are planned as the basic guides and resources in Christian education, but are not all that a church needs in the task. A wealth of books, magazines, audio-visual materials, art, maps, and other resources are available to supplement the basic texts. They can add immensely to the understanding of Christianity and one's part in it.

Much can be learned about a church and what it thinks about itself and its mission by listening to the hymns, anthems, and instrumental music it uses in corporate worship and in Christian education. A church must give critical attention to the music it presents to its people. Is the church growing in its appreciation of its musical heritage?

Reproductions of many great works of art are available at nominal cost. Even a small church with limited funds can acquire over a period of years a fine collection of reproductions for use in classes and for framing and hanging on the walls. These can be a most important resource to supplement the basic materials and to enrich the life of the church in which the teaching ministry takes place. The heritage of music and art is a part of the church today, and deserves recognition, appreciation, and enjoyment.

The symbolism and architecture of a church's own building—if it is worthy—can be valuable resources for Christian education. Are we making use of them? Do our people understand them? Are we mindful of them in worship? If the building was carefully designed it speaks of the faith of the people who learn, worship, and work there. Are we helping our people to be aware of this message and respond to it?

One church has a building of sufficient distinction that it has been written up in a book on the history of architecture. It is rich with symbolism, drawn deeply from the architecture of the ages. Yet few of the members of the church knew much about it. A minister who wanted to preach a sermon about the architecture, looked through the several histories of that church and found only passing reference to the architecture. Drawing from his own knowledge of the architecture of that building, and the history of church architecture, he preached the sermon.

The next Sunday one of the active members of the church came to him and said, "You made me almost have an accident." Puzzled, the minister asked how that could be. The man replied, "While I was driving up the street this morning I strained my neck to try to see those flying buttresses you told us about last Sunday, and almost ran into another car."

Other members walked around and through the church, seeing elements of its design they had never noticed before, and would not have understood had they seen them. Over the front door was a sculptured tympanum showing Jesus teaching his disciples. Many members said that they had been attending that church for years, passing under the tympanum without noticing it. Now they went outdoors and studied it. So with other details of the building, inside and outside.

Through the years a rich resource for enlarging the members' understanding of the history of Christianity had stood all about them, but they had been unaware, and no minister had called their attention to it.

Church leaders should realize that they can buy resource materials, as they can buy anthems and hymnbooks, but they cannot buy a curriculum, any more than they can buy corporate worship. Christian education happens in what the church does both inside the church building and beyond it, in the community and the world, in the atmosphere with which it surrounds its people, old and young, and in the Christian concern and love it expresses to those who come seeking. Curriculum comes into being from the inside of a church's life outward.

25 Everybody Teaches

Jim came home from church with a worried expression on his face. "Mom, why is the church going to fire Sam?"

"What makes you think the church is going to fire Sam, Jim?"

"I overheard a conversation between Mr. Johns and Mr. Cleveland today. Mr. Johns told Mr. Cleveland that Sam is getting old and isn't capable of being custodian any longer. Mr. Cleveland said it wasn't right to let him go without a pension because he has worked for the church nearly thirty years. Mr. Johns said the church had never started a pension fund for him and it was too late now —the church couldn't afford it."

"I'm sorry for Sam, too," said his mother. "He's been a good custodian for a long time. But Mr. Johns is a trustee, and I guess that the trustees know what they can do."

"Well, I don't think it is what a church ought to do. Sam is my friend. He's a friend of all the boys at the church. He knows me better than the minister does."

"Now Jim, don't talk that way."

"Well, it's true. What good is all that stuff they teach us in the church school if the trustees don't live up to it any better than that? I don't think I'll ever go back to that place again!"

What was the church teaching Jim? Who was teaching him and the other children and young people of the church? Everybody was, for better or for worse.

A minister from India (an Indian) was speaking at a meeting in America and said that it was not primarily the sermons preached nor the church school lessons taught in India that were causing people to turn to Christianity. What was doing it was the behavior of the Christian merchants that was different from that of the non-Christian merchants. It was the difference between the lives of the Christian doctor, dentist, businessman, neighbor and that of non-Christians that convinced people of the truth of the Christian gospel. So it is anywhere in the world.

Not all the behavior of so-called Christians is such that it convinces non-Christians that the gospel is true. Too often the Christian fails to respond to the gospel in his own life. His Christianity is a pretense; and its influence is negative.

Some members of a church became concerned about the relevance of Christianity in their social situation. They formed a study group to look more deeply into the meaning of their faith. They were convinced that Christ brought a message about God's creative and redemptive love for all mankind. They wanted to know if it is a gospel that says anything about the solution to the problems they face every day. Is it a gospel to which they could respond with commitment in the complex world situation in which they were caught? How could they respond to it in business?

The influence of the group spread within that church, and other study groups were formed. The effect of their serious concern about Christian responsibility throughout the week was felt by all the members, even the adults who did not participate in the study. The presence of those groups in the church gave a background of Christian concern and commitment that was of great help to the church school teachers and their students. Many of the members of those groups became teachers or resource leaders in the church school.

Regardless of what we say in the church school classroom, the students quickly see through the lives of the adults of the church, including their own parents, the church school teachers, and church officials. They measure the lives of adults against what is taught in Christian education. We cannot say to the appointed church school teachers, "You teach the children and young people how to be Christian while we take care of our own lives and the business of the church the way we have to do it in this rough-and-tumble pagan world."

Unless the adults of a church do the best they can to back up Christian education by seriously living up to the Christian message, they might almost as well not teach it at all. Boys and girls do not expect the adults of the church to be saints. They do expect, and have a right to expect, that adults will take the gospel as seriously in their own lives as they ask the students to take it in theirs.

Everybody in the church is a teacher, whether he likes it or not. A learning, witnessing, worshiping church is, constructively, a teaching church. A church engaged in its mission in its community and the world, dealing courageously with the issues of life, can draw children, young people, and new members into that work of mission and worship.

Let us not assume that Christian education takes place only during the church school session on Sunday. It goes on all week long. The church school has certain functions to carry out as part of the Christian education ministry of a church, and it is an extremely important part. But if the whole work of the church is not being done with sincerity, imagination, and commitment, the church school will have great difficulty carrying out its part effectively.

The growing child is on a journey from where he is at the moment into his larger life in the church, the community, and the world. It is a difficult and often confusing journey. The church school teacher, or other Christian education leader, has the responsibility for being his companion on that journey. The teacher does not provide the setting for the journey—the church, community, and family provide it. Whatever the setting, the student and teacher find themselves together in it. To help them understand the situation and make decisions regarding their own participation in it they have curriculum materials, resource materials, resource leaders, and the heritage of the church's art, music, history, scripture, and tradition. The situation is made for them by others. They can change it if they wish, or try to, by participating in it and working from the inside. There are many instances in which children and young people have brought about important changes in a church. If they like the situation they can support it, or they can change and support it selectively. They are never completely controlled by the situation in which they find themselves.

The adult members of a church, however, must realize that the dominant influence on a student is that situation with which they surround him and his teacher. The church itself and its work in the world, with whatever strengths and weaknesses are there, are the learning situation. The adult members create the learning situation, with all its limitations and possibilities. They are, therefore, teachers. What they are and do as Christians largely determines the outcome of what happens in the classrooms.

The most important part of a church's effort to achieve relevancy in the lives of its students, is the examination of itself as a church. What is the real essence of the church's work in the world—out where God is carrying on his age-long, almost impossible, but tremendously imaginative and determined creation? He is doing it with unbelievable patience and endurance, because most of the time we make the work difficult for him. How well are we, as people of the church, understanding our part in the world to which God is giving himself in a work in which he hopes we will join him? What does this understanding say in relation to what we do as a church and as individual Christians?

As we face these questions and let the church program grow out of our deliberations, we can turn to the examination of the part of our life usually called Christian education. We can recognize that although Christian education is much broader than what is done in the school, part of it does need to be carried on in some such situation as a church school. We may want to enlarge the school, or hold it during the week, or both on Sunday and during the week. We may feel that we need a professional, paid teaching staff, or we may renew our confidence in a volunteer staff. There are many changes we may make to contribute to the strengthening of what is done in the classroom.

Important as these changes may be, however, behind all the improvements must stand the recognition that the church itself, in its work and worship, is the primary teaching agent. This recognition has power in it if we are determined that the witness of the church shall be genuine, coming from the first-hand experience of people in seeking answers to the profound and primary questions, "Who are we? Why are we here? Where are we going? What is the meaning of it all? What is my responsibility? How do I operate as a human being and a Christian? What can I do about my life?"

Epilogue

Some readers of this book may wonder why more attention has not been given to new teaching procedures and methods of Christian education. Suggestions along those lines are available in other books,* and the author sees the purpose of this book as encouraging churches to take a fresh look at what they are doing in Christian education in a revolutionary time. The world about them is in a period of extremely rapid change and development. Any institution, to be relevant in such a time, must carry on a constant and running re-examination of its reason for being and of its actions in the light of that reason.

This book has been designed to be used as a way of opening and expanding a church's thinking about its Christian education responsibility rather than circumscribing it. Many situations in which learning can take place that have been touched on only in passing should receive careful attention by a church.

Only brief mention has been made of a development that is far from casual: /the growing ecumenical consciousness and activity of churches, not only in relation to each other but to the whole range of political, economic, and social revolution. This activity is carried on at many levels: international, national, area, and local. One of the local opportunities for involvement in this engagement is being provided, for example, in ecumenical dialogues. As local churches come to know each other better there will be increasing possibilities of local ecumenical action in the development of curriculum and

---

* For such suggestions see Eleanor S. Morrison and Virgil E. Foster, *Creative Teaching in the Church* (Englewood Cliffs, N.J.: Prentice-Hall, Inc., 1963). Paperback and cloth.

of learning situations that are free from the inhibitions and limitations of a parochial educational approach.

Mention has been made of educational centers and conferences. But the possibilities of dynamic learning experiences through lay institutes and training centers; the many conferences, seminars, and forums carried on by churches and many other agencies of the community and nation; and the wide range of church conferences and conventions merit much more attention from Christian education leaders than they are receiving.

Brief references have been made to mass media of communication and the audio-visual and electronic equipment and materials being developed. The educational possibilities in these areas are far greater than has been explored in this book, and they deserve careful scrutiny and planning by every local church. Some plays, motion pictures, television programs, and radio programs, for example, lift up crucial issues confronting people. These can provide the opening for significant study, discussion, and action by church groups. They are a resource provided at no cost to the churches, and their value is beyond calculation. There is also rapid development in electronic, mechanical, and printed media especially for use in the church's educational ministry.

References have been made to family responsibility in Christian education, but these have not dealt with the pressures on families from within and without, and the changes in family life they bring about. These are thought of too often only as presenting problems, but they present opportunities, too. Every change, every new pressure, every accomplishment brings with it a dynamic opportunity for learning. Some families desperately need the help of churches. Others are far out ahead of the churches in their educational accomplishments. In the re-examination of its educational ministry every church should be enlightened about its families and forthright in recognizing the team responsibility of church and home in Christian education.

In like manner, there are many other areas in which learning takes place, sometimes for good and sometimes for ill. A church should be aware of them and take them under careful consideration as it appraises its opportunities for education and plans for its educational ministry. If this book accomplishes its purpose its contribution will mark for some churches the beginning of re-examination and expansion of their educational effort; for others it will be only a nudge in an appraisal already well under way. Churches can well afford to close out programs that are ineffective or obsolete, in order to carry their educational ministry into the areas where learning is already taking place or can most surely be caused to take place. The world's invitation to undertake such a venture is pressing.

Index